THE HUNDRED YEARS WAR

British History in Perspective
General Editor: Jeremy Black

THE HUNDRED YEARS WAR

ANNE CURRY

Lecturer in History
University of Reading

First published 1993 by
THE MACMILLAN PRESS LTD
Houndmills, Basingstoke, Hampshire RG21 2XS
and London
Companies and representatives
throughout the world

ISBN 0–333–53175–2 hardcover
ISBN 0–333–53176–0 paperback

A catalogue record for this book is available
from the British Library.

Typeset by Footnote Graphics,
Warminster, Wiltshire

Printed in Hong Kong

Series Standing Order

If you would like to receive future titles in this series as they are
published, you can make use of our standing order facility. To place a
standing order please contact your bookseller or, in case of difficulty,
write to us at the address below with your name and address and the
name of the series. Please state with which title you wish to begin your
standing order. (If you live outside the United Kingdom we may not
have the rights for your area, in which case we will forward your order
to the publisher concerned.)

Customer Services Department, Macmillan Distribution Ltd
Houndmills, Basingstoke, Hampshire, RG21 2XS, England.

CONTENTS

PREFACE

This book owes much to the hard work and enthusiasm of fellow historians on both sides of the Channel. In particular, I would like to thank Professor J. S. Roskell for first alerting me to the fascination of the subject, and Professor C. T. Allmand and Dr A. J. Pollard for guiding my research. Of my colleagues, Professors M. D. Biddiss and B. R. Kemp deserve special mention for their helpful advice in the preparation of this book. John and Tom have had to put up with much neglect on the home front, but have never ceased to provide support and encouragement. To them I offer both my love and my gratitude.

Flanders

CALAIS

Ponthieu

Channel
Islands

'ROUEN

PARIS

REIMS

Normandy

Brittany

Maine

Anjou

Touraine

Poitou

LA ROCHELLE

Saintonge

The Three
Dioceses
(limited rights
only)

Auvergne

Approximate extent of
English-held lands 1327

Lands granted or promised
by the Treaty of Paris 1259

Angevin domination at its
greatest extent, late
twelfth century

BORDEAUX

Agenais

Quercy

Gascony

County of
Toulouse

BAYONNE

Armagnac

Bearn
Bigorre

English lands in France before 1327

English lands by the Treaty of Brétigny, 1360

The extent of English control of France in the fifteenth century

The European context

Fl – Flanders
Br – Brabant
Ha – Hainault
— – western boundary of imperial authority

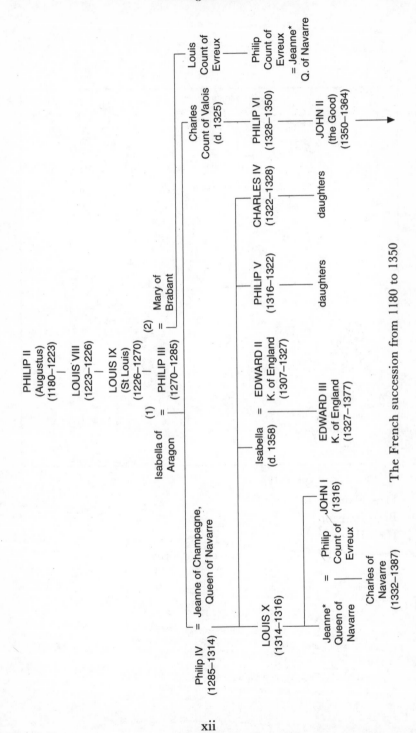

The French succession from 1180 to 1350

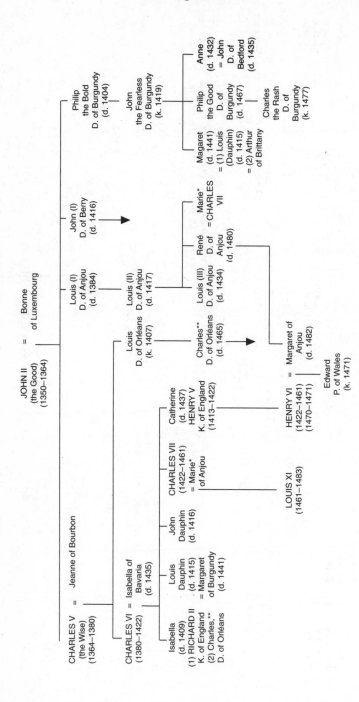

French kings from 1350 to 1483

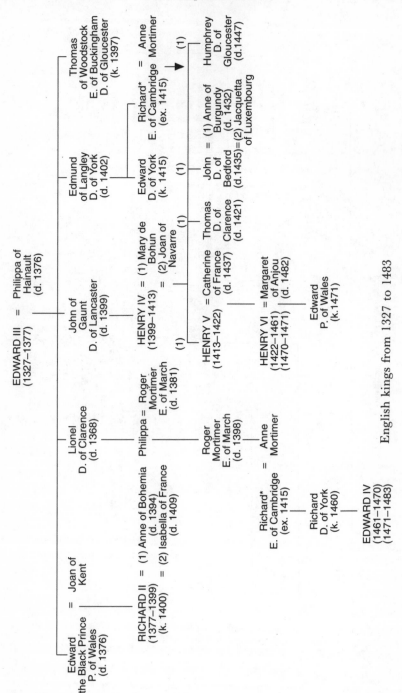

EDWARD III = Philippa of Hainault
(1327–1377)   (d. 1376)

Edward the Black Prince P. of Wales (d. 1376) = Joan of Kent

RICHARD II (1377–1399) (k. 1400) = (1) Anne of Bohemia (d. 1394) = (2) Isabella of France (d. 1409)

Lionel D. of Clarence (d. 1368)

Philippa = Roger Mortimer E. of March (d. 1381)

Roger Mortimer E. of March (d. 1398)

Anne Mortimer = Richard* E. of Cambridge (ex. 1415)

Richard D. of York (k. 1460)

EDWARD IV (1461–1470) (1471–1483)

John of Gaunt D. of Lancaster (d. 1399)

HENRY IV (1399–1413) = (1) Mary de Bohun = (2) Joan of Navarre

HENRY V (1413–1422) = Catherine of France (d. 1437)

Thomas D. of Clarence (d. 1421)

HENRY VI (1422–1461) (1470–1471) = Margaret of Anjou (d. 1482)

Edward P. of Wales (k.1471)

Edmund of Langley D. of York (d. 1402)

Richard* E. of Cambridge (ex. 1415) = Anne Mortimer

Edward D. of York (k. 1415)

John D. of Bedford (d.1435) = (1) Anne of Burgundy (d. 1432) = (2) Jacquetta of Luxembourg

Thomas of Woodstock E. of Buckingham D. of Gloucester (k. 1397)

Humphrey D. of Gloucester (d.1447)

English kings from 1327 to 1483

INTRODUCTION

One of the first things students learn about the Hundred Years War is that it lasted 116 years – from 1337, when Philip VI confiscated the French lands of Edward III, to 1453, when English Gascony fell to the French. The starting and finishing dates present immediate problems. The English and French had been at war on many occasions before 1337, indeed, as recently as 1327. They were to be in conflict again many times after 1453. Much of the subsequent history of this country concerns its struggle with France, both in Europe and in the wider world. Historians have even postulated the existence of a 'second Hundred Years War' lasting from 1689 to 1815.

In terms of English landed interests in France, the period from 1337 to 1453 is likewise not unique. Since the Norman Conquest English kings had ruled various territories in France.[1] Until its loss in 1204, the duchy of Normandy was almost always in the hands of the king of England. So, too, were Anjou and Maine, from the accession of their count to the throne of England as Henry II in 1154 to their loss under his son, King John, in 1204–5. In 1152 Henry married Eleanor, heiress to the great duchy of Aquitaine, which included the county of Poitou. These lands thus came into the hands of Henry II and his royal successors. Poitou briefly fell to the French under John but was not finally lost until 1224. Thenceforward the territorial holdings of the English kings were restricted to a much truncated duchy of Aquitaine, usually called Gascony or Guienne. In 1279 the county of Ponthieu, straddling the Somme, came to the crown through Edward I's queen. The landed interests of English kings in France were thus substantial well before 1337. As for ending the Hundred Years War with the loss of Gascony in 1453, we must remember that Calais (captured by Edward III in 1347) remained in English hands until 1558.

The holding of lands in France had given rise to conflicts with the kings of France on several occasions before 1337. There were clashes before the time of Philip (Augustus) II (1180–1223), but perhaps his reign should be taken as a major turning point. It began with the French possessions of the English kings at their greatest extent. It then saw the first real attempts by the French to conquer these lands by force of arms. And, more importantly, it witnessed the first full exploitation of French feudal overlordship in order to achieve this conquest. English kings were sovereign in their kingdom, but they held their French lands as dukes or counts. Thus they had a superior lord – the king of France – to whom they owed homage. Feudal custom gave the superior lord various powers over his vassal. Not least, he could declare confiscate his vassal's lands if he considered that the latter had acted against his own will as lord. This is what Philip II did in 1202. In the wars which ensued, as we have seen, the English king lost much of his territory in France. There was no peace settlement until 1259, when Henry III and Louis IX agreed to the Treaty of Paris. This restored to Henry some of the lost lands of Aquitaine, but in return he formally gave up claims to Normandy, Anjou, Maine and Poitou. He also accepted his obligation to pay liege homage for Aquitaine.

This treaty did not bring lasting peace. Under Edward I (1272–1307) the exercise of French overlordship, the payment of homage and the geographical extent of English possessions became major issues. They led to French kings confiscating Aquitaine and Ponthieu in 1294 and 1324. On both occasions this caused war between England and France. Neither these wars nor the peace treaties which ended them (1303 and 1327) really solved any of the issues. In May 1337 Philip VI of France confiscated the French possessions of Edward III: England and France were again at war. This, as we have seen, is the beginning of what has become known as the Hundred Years War. What was it that made this war different from any of the previous Anglo-French conflicts? What makes 1337 the beginning of a new stage in Anglo-French relations, a stage which has been seen as lasting to 1453?

The answer is Edward III's claim to the French throne. Even here, however, there are problems with dates. The main French (Capetian) royal line had come to an end in 1328. Edward's advisers certainly put forward his candidature then, as the son of Isabella, sister of the last three French kings. Yet no war for the crown then ensued. The count of Valois, heir through the male line, became king of France as Philip VI, and Edward duly paid homage to him for his French lands. Philip VI confiscated Edward's French lands in May 1337 and the two kingdoms were thus once more at war. Edward did not put forward a formal claim to the French throne until 26 January 1340, when he assumed the title 'King of France' at Ghent. If the Hundred Years War is seen as the struggle between English and French claimants for the throne of France, then there is a strong argument for seeing 1340 as the real turning point in Anglo-French relations rather than 1337. We are now at the heart of the matter. Was the war which Edward III and his successors waged against France a feudal or a dynastic war? Was it caused by problems arising out of the tenure of lands in France, much as previous wars had been, or was it a bid to gain the throne of France?

There are no simple answers to these questions, as will become clear in the subsequent chapters of this book. During the period of Anglo-French warfare from 1340 to 1360 Edward called himself king of France. In the Treaty of Brétigny of 1360 he gave up the title in return for sovereignty in Aquitaine, Poitou, Ponthieu and Calais. In theory, then, both the feudal and the dynastic issues were solved at Brétigny. Yet war broke out again in 1369 when, claiming to be feudal overlord as his predecessors had been, Charles V of France confiscated Edward's lands. In response Edward once again claimed to be rightful king of France, as did his successors. No full settlement could be reached, although a 28-year truce was agreed in 1396. In 1415

Henry V began a series of successful campaigns in France. The Treaty of Troyes (1420) named him as heir to the throne of France, but as he predeceased Charles VI, it was his son, Henry VI, who became king of France by virtue of the Troyes settlement. War continued with the rival claimant, Charles VI's son, Charles VII, who had been disinherited by his father as a necessary corollary of the Troyes settlement. The English never succeeded in controlling the whole of France. In 1436 they lost Paris. Between 1449 and 1453 Charles VII took Normandy and then Gascony, leaving only Calais in English hands.

Should 1453 be seen as the end of an era? Never again did English kings hold such wide dominions in France. Yet Anglo-French hostilities persisted after 1453. Moreover, the claim to the French throne still stood. All subsequent rulers called themselves kings (or queens) of France. They only stopped doing so at the point of negotiating the Treaty of Amiens with Napoleon in 1801-2. There is some irony that the claim was abandoned only when France had killed its king and had fallen under the rule of a man of plebeian stock who was soon to claim imperial status. Thirteen years later, however, the armies of the English king at Waterloo scored perhaps their greatest victory against the French since Agincourt (1415), thereby assisting the restoration of a French monarchy in France. To complete the irony, the 'second Hundred Years War' ended with the English gaining the victory which had eluded them in the first.

There has been considerable debate about the causes of the Hundred Years War. The central question is whether it was fought over the long-standing issues arising out of the tenure of lands in France or over who should be king of France. When first contemplating the organisation of this book, I thought that it would be best to take these two issues separately, tracing each over the entire course of the war. As I investigated the topic it soon became clear that this demarcation would not do. The issues are so closely intertwined that to separate them would be misleading. It is clear that there was not one single 'hundred year' war. Fighting was not continuous; there were many periods of truce and, between 1360 and 1369, there was in theory full peace. War aims and methods changed over time, according to circumstances and personalities in both countries. It seemed best, therefore, to treat the subject chronologically. Chapters 2 and 3 take the form of a 'narrative with commentary' as a means of examining English objectives and actions in the various stages of Anglo-French conflict. The Hundred Years War raises many issues beyond those of causes and events. One important aspect is that the struggle was never simply between England and France. The European dimension is of crucial importance. The role of Scotland demands close examination for her 'auld alliance' with France was a significant factor in the wars and in the survival of Scotland as an independent nation. This wider context is discussed in chapter 4.

If the approach of this book needs to be categorised then it should perhaps be placed under 'international relations'. What it endeavours to provide is a succinct and fairly basic review of Anglo-French relations in the later middle ages for those with little previous knowledge of the subject. It is a diplomatic rather than a military study, focusing particularly on war aims and on attempts to effect a settlement. It is not intended as, nor would its length permit it to be, a full narrative of the war. After all, the complexity of events is such that it has recently taken Jonathan Sumption over 600 pages merely to treat of the war to 1347.[2] This book concentrates mainly on an English perspective of the wars, but says little about the impact of war on politics, economy or society. For these one must look to other works.[3] Indeed, the Hundred Years War has received much attention from historians both past and present. Before commencing our discussion of events it is helpful to have some idea of the historiography of the subject. It is, then, to the historians of the war that we turn first.

1

THE HUNDRED YEARS WAR AND HISTORIANS

The 'Hundred Years War' is, strictly speaking, an invention of historians. The phrase 'Guerre de Cent Ans' first occurs in print in France in 1861, and was soon taken up with enthusiasm in England.[1] Thenceforward the term has enjoyed universal acceptance in popular and academic circles alike. By the time it was coined much ink had already been expended on the Anglo-French conflicts of the later middle ages. Even within the period itself, the wars formed the predominant subject of many narratives, and these in turn provided the principal materials for historians of subsequent centuries. Thus there is much to read, even if some of it, both medieval and later, is blatantly derivative or prejudiced. In this study we can outline only the main themes of the subject's historiography. As we shall see, many influences played on those who wrote about the wars in the past: the sources at their disposal; their patriotic or political sympathies; their purpose in writing; their expected audience; and the view of 'history' which obtained at the time of writing.

Contemporary Chroniclers

By modern definition, all who wrote about the wars at the time they were happening were biased. This was partly because of what they saw the purpose of historical writing to be – the recording for posterity of the events of their own lifetime. With such a view they could not fail to be influenced by their personal situation. Not surprisingly, writers show a distinctly national bias. English chroniclers (a more appropriate term than historians), and European chroniclers such as Froissart who wrote for English or pro-English patrons and audiences, obviously stressed the rightness of the English cause and concentrated on the periods of English success. In some cases, works seem to have been commissioned for a specific purpose. The *Gesta Henrici Quinti*, for example, was probably written in 1416–17 to justify in England and at the Council of Constance Henry V's invasions of France both past and intended. Here Henry was portrayed as a model Christian prince. By emphasising Henry's success both against heretics in England and against the French, God was revealed as being unequivocally on the side of the English. That does not mean, however, that the *Gesta* provides an inaccurate narrative of what actually happened on the Agincourt campaign; in fact, very much the contrary, for its author seems to be a reliable eyewitness.[2]

The period from 1337 to 1453 saw a large number of chroniclers at work in both England and France, and for that matter, elsewhere in Europe.[3] My discussion concerns for the most part pro-English sources, but comparisons and similarities will be drawn with their French counterparts whenever possible.

All chroniclers tended to be most interested in the doings of kings and nobles. It is not surprising, therefore, that Anglo-French relations and military activity should figure prominently in the writings of the period. For some chroniclers, however, the conflict was only one theme amongst many. Monastic chroniclers such as Thomas Walsingham, writing at St Albans between c.1380 and 1422, were composing general narratives of events in a well-worn, but by now declining tradition, and would have done so even if the wars had not taken place. This is probably true also of the largely anonymous London chroniclers who produced the *Brut* and the Chronicles of London. It has been suggested that the change of language of these London writers from French to English towards the end of the fourteenth century was due to the sense of national identity which the French wars had strengthened. This is clearly an oversimplistic explanation of the complex issues surrounding the rapid rise of written English in the period. None the less, the style and content of these chronicles – texts of which are very numerous for the fifteenth century and which, as we shall see, provide a direct link with the historians of the sixteenth century – do demonstrate strong xenophobia against the French. One of the best known examples of this is the description of the furore in the city after the defection of the duke of Burgundy from the English cause in 1435. The strongly anti-Burgundian and anti-Flemish stance is explained by the fears of London's mercantile lobby that their trading interests with Burgundian-controlled Flanders would be irretrievably damaged. The *Brut*, not surprisingly, gives a detailed account of Burgundy's abortive siege of Calais in 1436, for the raising of which the city of London contributed both men and money.[4]

Chronicles can reveal, then, something of popular reaction to the war as well as the extent and reception of royal propaganda. The London chronicles, and indeed all of the fourteenth- and fifteenth-century narratives under discussion here, frequently include, either verbatim or in summary, documents emanating from the crown. These include proclamations and manifestos against the French. Adam Murimuth, for instance, gives the full text of an agreement between Philip VI and his Norman vassals dated 23 March 1338, drawn up in anticipation of an invasion of England. This document had apparently been discovered at Edward III's sacking of Caen in August 1346. It was carried back to England by the earl of Huntingdon, who had been invalided home, for public reading by the archbishop of Canterbury at the customary venue of Saint Paul's Churchyard, with the express purpose that the English should be excited by this proof of French malevolence to support the king's war even more avidly. Before and after this text, Murimuth includes copies of four newsletters detailing Edward III's military successes since his landing at St Vaast la Hougue on 12 July 1346. Newsletters from the front are found in many chronicles of the war period – Robert of Avesbury's *De Gestis Mirabilibus Edwardi Tertii*, for instance, is little more than a series of newsletters and other official texts interspersed with a bare narrative – and they are so plentiful for the reign of Edward III that Prince concluded that they represent 'a rudimentary publicity system' for the crown and its captains.[5] It was also common for chroniclers to give the texts of peace treaties: the Treaty of Troyes (1420), for instance, is included in the *Great Chronicle of London* in the version which was ordered to be proclaimed in the city, in the *Chronique du Religieux de Saint Denis* as agreed at the meeting of the kings at Troyes, and in the chronicles of Monstrelet, Waurin and Le Fèvre as ordered to be published in Paris.[6] The practice of including texts in chronicles was not new, and indeed documents of other sorts and on other subjects are found, such as those of ecclesiastical provenance. What we can see, however, is something of the way chroniclers gleaned their information as well as of how the government sought to inform and influence the population as a whole. In this respect we read in these chronicles what the crown wanted its subjects to know about the war.

There was, however, no tradition of an official court chronicler in England during the wars or earlier, although there is a strong suspicion that Robert of Avesbury's *De Gestis Mirabilibus Edwardi Tertii* and the anonymous *Gesta Henrici Quinti* may have been written at the behest of the respective monarchs. In France, the monastery of Saint-Denis produced both Latin and French chronicles for the kings of the fourteenth and early fifteenth centuries but ceased to do so after the death of Charles VI (1422), perhaps because the crown was then contested between Henry VI of England and Charles VII. Molinier suggests that the wars undermined French monarchical centralisation, thus allowing 'la resurrection de l'historiographie locale'. He adds that the theatre of military operations became so vast that no single general chronicler could have written accurately or comprehensively on the wars.[7] As a result, much French chronicling of the wars in both centuries was locally based.

Of particular interest are those chronicles which were written either wholly or partly because of the Anglo-French wars. We have seen this already for the *Gesta Henrici Quinti*. Later, but equally eulogistic, lives of Henry V were probably commissioned to revive enthusiasm for the English war effort: in the mid 1430s by Humphrey, duke of Gloucester, the king's last surviving brother and outspoken opponent of peace moves; in the mid 1440s by Walter, Lord Hungerford, steward of Henry V's household; and even as late as 1513, when Henry VIII was seeking to emulate his illustrious namesake. On the chroniclers of Edward III's reign, Gransden suggests that 'it is probable that England's resounding victories provided an incentive to historical compilation'. It cannot be a coincidence, for instance, that both the Lanercost chronicler and Adam of Murimuth end with the English victory over the Scots at Nevilles Cross in 1346, shortly after the defeat of the French at Crécy, that Geoffrey Le Baker terminates at the battle of Poitiers (1356) with the terse remark that the desired peace was not forthcoming over the next two years, and that Robert of Avesbury ends shortly before Poitiers but includes lists of those killed or captured at the battle.[8] The wars with the French and the Scots much affected all these writers. Le Baker gives much military detail, particularly on the Black Prince's activities, although he confuses the various Breton campaigns. Murimuth includes the fullest justification of Edward III's claim to the French throne complete with family tree, but later adds a note of criticism on Edward's excessive and unprecedented demands for war finance.[9] Although they were all secular clerks who wrote in Latin, they accept without question the chivalric and patriotic values of crown and nobility. This is most obvious in Avesbury, whose introductory section emphasises his intention to record the great deeds of Edward and his nobility in England, Scotland, France, Aquitaine and Brittany, and whose work includes little not germane to the war.[10]

Murimuth and Le Baker had begun their works in the reign of Edward II and were more in the tradition of the generalist monastic chroniclers. Their works do not owe their existence to the wars in the same way as do, for the fourteenth century, the works of the Hainaulters Jean Le Bel and Jean Froissart, the Chandos herald (who wrote a verse Life of the Black Prince) and Sir Thomas Gray (author of the *Scalacronica*), or for the fifteenth century, the works of the Burgundians, Enguerran de Monstrelet and Jean de Waurin, and the chronicle of Peter Basset and Christopher Hanson. All of these men wrote in French.

Froissart is by far the best known, both in his own lifetime and thereafter, and there has been much academic debate over the nature, sources and reliability of his works.[11] The content of his voluminous output was heavily influenced by whatever royal or aristocratic audience he was writing for and was revised accordingly. His first work, now lost, seems to have been an account 'of the wars and adventures' of Edward III from the battle of Poitiers to 1360, written for Edward III's queen. The first redaction of his *Chroniques*, under the patronage of Robert of Namur, Edward III's ally and relative by marriage, is very pro-English; the second, written in the 1380s and 90s when Froissart was associated with the pro-French Wenceslaus of Bohemia and Guy of Blois, is much more sympathetic to the French. However, the overall rationale behind his work – the desire to record great deeds of great men – never changed. The prologue to the first redaction of the *Chroniques* shows clearly this intention in the context of the wars:

> In order that the honourable enterprises, noble adventures and deeds of arms which took place during the wars waged by France and England should be fittingly related and preserved for posterity, so that brave men should be inspired thereby to follow such examples, I wish to place on record these matters of great renown.[12]

His *Chroniques* are thus not so much a history of the Anglo-French wars as an account of the great deeds of the royal and noble participants. This is, of course, precisely what his similarly composed audience wished to hear, even though, as Taylor comments, 'his love of realistic detail often led him to describe episodes somewhat in variance with the chivalric ideal'.[13] As Froissart was himself a secular clerk and never an eyewitness or participant in the wars, save perhaps in the Flemish campaign of 1383, he relied upon the reminiscences of the knightly group. He also drew upon information kept by the heralds: it seems likely, for instance, that he used material compiled by the herald of Sir John Chandos in advance of the latter's composition of his life of the Black Prince. The significance of the heralds in the context of chronicling the Anglo-French wars should not be under-estimated. Developing their functions from the minstrels with whom they had been linked before the wars began, they listed battle presences, brave deeds and mortalities. These could then be drawn upon by other writers; Monstrelet, for instance, cites kings of arms, heralds and pursuivants of all lands and countries 'who by virtue of their office ought to be fair and diligent inquirers ... and true relaters'. On occasion, heralds themselves turn their hands to chronicle composition, as in the case of the fifteenth-century Frenchmen, Jean Le Fèvre de Saint-Rémy, and of Gilles Le Bouvier, otherwise known as the Berry herald, whose account of the expulsion of the English from Normandy is of particular interest and value.[14]

Other chronicles stimulated by the war are similar to Froissart both in tone and in the nature of their sources. In the case of Jean Le Bel this is not surprising given that Froissart extensively used the chronicle of his fellow Hainaulter and secular clerk for his own narrative in 1361. Le Bel, too, wanted to record the deeds of the noble and valorous, but in accurate fashion without the exaggeration of the older poetic tradition. In this respect, Le Bel set the precedent of the French prose chivalric chronicle. Pro-English – his patron, John of Hainault, was Queen Philippa's uncle and actively involved in Edward III's early Scottish and French campaigns – he was the first to establish the French wars of Edward III and Philip VI as something particularly worthy of record, and thus by implication a new departure in Anglo-French relations in which the palm of victory and of valour was to be accorded to the English king.[15] His views have become well known by virtue of Froissart's dependence upon them, although the latter gives even more on the actions of Edward at the outset of the wars and beyond.

The Burgundian chroniclers Monstrelet and Waurin are also highly interdependent – no one has yet established their exact relationship – and change their pro-English stance once the Anglo-Burgundian alliance comes to an end in 1435. They also outline in their prologues a similar intention to record the deeds of the valorous as both a commemoration and an example to be followed. Monstrelet states his desire to be a continuator of

Froissart and begins where the latter left off in 1400: Waurin
expresses surprise that no English writers have recorded the
deeds of their kings and princes save in 'little books on each king
individually'.[16] Their intentions do not prevent either of these
chronicles being of vital assistance in the reconstruction of events
and, even more importantly, of attitudes. Both Waurin and
Monstrelet are of special interest to us as serving soldiers who
subsequently turned to writing chronicles. Waurin was present
at Agincourt and at later actions: Monstrelet was probably
captain of Frévent in Picardy for the Burgundian count of St
Pol.[17] The writing of chronicles by soldiers was not a new
phenomenon but it was much stimulated by the Anglo-French
wars and by the growth of lay literacy, both being distinctive
features of the later middle ages. Sir Thomas Gray, a knight of
Northumberland who saw military service against the Scots and
under the Black Prince in France, provides us in the *Scalacronica*
with what are essentially his memoirs, the title being derived
from his family sign of a ladder. The work is imbued throughout
with the chivalric views of its author and, like that of Froissart,
proves Ainsworth's observation that 'medieval texts knew of no
sharp distinction between literature and fiction, romance, history and chronicle'.[18]

The details of the military service of Sir John Chandos's
herald are not known, but his life of the Black Prince, unusual
for being in the declining genre of French verse, is composed
not as a chronicle but as a didactic eulogy of two models of
knighthood, the Black Prince and Sir John Chandos. In this it
has parallels with the roughly contemporary verse life of the
French war hero, Bertrand du Guesclin.[19] The didactic element
is worth stressing for the herald's work may have been composed
for the prince's son, Richard II, in the hope that the young king
would emulate his father's achievements in France. The chronicle of soldiers Basset and Hanson covers the war from 1415 to
1429, and exists only in a single manuscript copy in the College
of Arms: it too may have had a didactic as well as a commemora-
tive function. Its preface indicates that it was written in collaboration with William Worcester, secretary to Sir John Fastolf who
had seen extensive service in France under Henry V and VI.

Worcester compiled other materials on the war for his master, composing too the *Boke of Noblesse*, which was intended to inspire Henry VI and later Edward IV to restore English glories in France. Basset and Hanson served in the wars. They, like Worcester, seem to have drawn upon the heralds' records, for their chronicle is of a very distinctive kind. Within the framework of a bare narrative of events, it gives lengthy lists of English and French men of rank, or of those who showed particular military prowess in engagements and in the captaincy of garrisons.[20]

In coming to conclusions about contemporary narratives of the Anglo-French conflict, we can be in no doubt that these wars, and the Scottish wars of Edward III before them, stimulated a new form of historical composition – the 'chivalric chronicle' written in the language of chivalry, French. On a few occasions the writings focus primarily on the deeds of one notable individual, often of royal blood. But in general these works reflect the mentality, and commemorate the activities, of the whole military elite, not only those who were noble but also those who achieved a form of nobility through military service – an opportunity for social advancement which was offered on a hitherto unprecedented scale in the Anglo-French wars. As Monstrelet stressed in his prologue, he wished to record the deeds of *all* the valiant, both those of noble lineage and those of low estate. Some of these writers were blatantly partisan in their favouring of one nation. From Froissart and Le Bel derives the notion of new-found English greatness, which has coloured many subsequent writings on the Hundred Years War. For Le Bel, for instance, the English had no reputation as warriors when Edward took the throne, but once they had taken arms under him they became the most noble and most *frisques* combatants then known.[21] Despite the patriotism of these works, it was none the less acceptable, indeed expected, for authors to cite the valours of the enemy's military elite too. This was encouraged by the supranational function of the heralds which led them to record the battle presences and feats of arms of both sides. This aspect is particularly evident in the work of Basset and Hanson, and in the narratives by Blondel and the Berry herald concerning the reconquest of Normandy by the French in 1449–50. Chronicles, therefore, have presented ensuing generations with a distinctive picture of a chivalric rather than a national war, which many later historians have been eager – sometimes overeager – to follow. For John Speed, writing in 1611, for instance,

the honor of the warre in those ages cannot bee enough commended in which the noble old forms of hostility were put into practice by defiances, heralds and public assignation of day and place of fight, and not by skulking surprises and underhand stealthes more neerly resembling high-way robberies than lawful battell.[22]

The most extreme manifestation of this view must be that of the early nineteenth-century historian, Hallam, when he wrote that the war of Edward III and the Black Prince

was like a great tournament, where the combatants fought indeed à *outrance* but with all the courtesy and fair play of such an entertainment, and almost as much for the honour of their ladies.[23]

The readability and romance of Froissart have ensured his lasting influence. In addition, lavishly illustrated copies of his text and of those of Monstrelet were made in the course of the later fifteenth century, and these continue to seduce the compilers of coffee-table books on the Hundred Years War even though their visual portrayal of war is often rather anachronistic. Chronicles were written for a specific purpose and with a specific outlook and do not necessarily tell the whole truth. They mislead on the size of armies and say little about defensive activity. As Sumption points out, they include next to nothing on naval actions, which modern historians now see as much more extensive and important to the way the wars unfolded, because they were fought by men of lower status outside the conventions of chivalry.[24] Yet without the chronicles we would miss so much of the excitement which the Anglo-French wars generated, and hence would find it impossible to explain why they happened or why men were prepared to risk their lives fighting them.

The Sixteenth Century

The chronicles provide the most important, often the only, sources for subsequent historians. Indeed, it is difficult to say when chronicling ends and historical writing on the wars begins. Some chroniclers wrote long after the events they describe. French chroniclers such as Basin, Blondel and the Berry herald dealt with the English occupation of Normandy in full knowledge that the French had finally won, thus their narratives tend to imply that this victory was both inevitable and longed for. Many of the London chronicles of the later fifteenth century were redrafts and compilations of earlier works so that it is not easy to distinguish them from the histories written in early sixteenth-century London by Robert Fabyan, John Stowe, Edward Hall and Raphael Holinshed. These later authors drew extensively on earlier chronicles, particularly the *Brut* which had been printed by Caxton in 1480.

It can be argued that the first real 'history' was that of the Italian cleric, Polydore Vergil. His *Historia Angliae* (first edition Basel, 1534) covers the whole of English history, and is thus the first single work to include the fourteenth- as well as the fifteenth-century wars. Polydore consulted many English and foreign chronicles, but he then endeavoured 'to compare the facts and weigh the statements of his predecessors'.[25] His work was translated into English before the death of Henry VIII but it seems to have been its Latin version which became well known and thus formed the basis of later sixteenth-century and subsequent histories, often predominating over, or at least enjoying equal status with, works written within the period of the wars themselves. Many later works, for instance, copy Polydore's reign-based format whereby a narrative is followed by a summary of each monarch's character. Here Polydore, much influenced by the humanists' rediscovery of the Classics, was emulating the style of Suetonius' *Lives of the Twelve Caesars*. He also attempted to come to judgements on why events had happened as they did. His pro-English stance coloured his views, so that, for instance, he considered that the loss of Aquitaine in 1453 should 'be attributed not so muche to the force as the falshood of the

16

Frenche'. But his was not the blind chivalric patriotism of the chroniclers. He emphasised the connection in the early 1450s between defeat in France and civil unrest at home: 'when forreine war was finished, intestine division began to revive; for a great part of the nobilitie fretted and fumed for the evill handling of matters in France...'. He suggested that the growing political divisions in England in the late 1440s had encouraged the rebellion of the Normans and Aquitanians against their English rulers. He may have been the first to voice the opinion that foreign war had helped to keep the English nobility in check, a notion which many later historians have accepted.[26]

The dominance of Froissart in any historical work which treated of the fourteenth century was made complete by its recommendation by Caxton, its early printing in France (1495), and its translation and printing in English by Lord Berners in 1523–5. Early printings of Monstrelet in France in both full and abridged form ensured a similar dominance for this fifteenth-century source.[27] Both were certainly consulted for Edward Hall's *Union of the Two Houses of York and Lancaster* (c.1532). Basset's chronicle also features in the list of authors from whom Hall claimed his work was 'first gathered, and after compiled and conioyned'. He gives Basset's first name incorrectly and does not mention Hanson, but there can be no doubt that Hall consulted the manuscript because most of his narrative of the period from 1415 to 1429 is taken from this source – lists of battle presences, captaincies and all.[28]

Then, of course, there is Shakespeare. Much ink has been spilt on the question of his historical sources but a direct link with contemporary chronicles through the printed texts of Fabyan, Hall, Stowe and Holinshed is well attested.[29] It appears from a reading of *Henry V* (1599) and *Henry VI, Part I* (1591–2) that the playwright was better informed about the wars of the former compared with those of the latter, partly because he was able to draw upon an existing play, *The Famous Victories of Henry V* (1593). The chronology and personnel of the war scenes in *Henry VI* are confused, and even in *Henry V* the period from 1415 to 1420 is conflated (as it was in the *Famous Victories*), but Shakespeare would not be the first or the last writer to skew fact for the sake of dramatic potential, or to make it relate to contemporary situations. In *Henry VI, Part I*, Act III, scene ii, the inaccurate notion that Rouen was lost to Joan of Arc and then retaken in a day may be an allusion to the sending of an army under the earl of Essex to help Henry of Navarre at the siege of Rouen in the summer of 1591. Shakespeare also sets the origins of the Wars of the Roses very firmly in the context of the rivalry between York and Somerset over command in France, but places it much earlier in the wars than either Polydore Vergil or Hall had done. What is equally interesting is the influence which Shakespeare has had on later historians. Following the revival of interest in the plays in the nineteenth and twentieth centuries, many popular accounts of the Hundred Years War used Shakespeare as a source in his own right, as a brief glance at Sir Winston Churchill's *History of the English Speaking Peoples* reveals: the proof that Henry was valorous is therein the first two lines of 'once more into the breach'. Churchill's equally illustrious ancestor, the first duke of Marlborough, claimed that Shakespeare was 'the only history I ever read'. Even today the plays remain central to popular conceptions of the Anglo-French wars.[30]

Can we deduce, then, a distinctive Tudor view on the Anglo-French wars of the fourteenth and fifteenth centuries? To a great extent the chivalric tone of the chroniclers persisted, not surprisingly given that they formed such an important source. Nor had audiences changed much. Histories were still compiled for aristocratic and royal consumption, and the cult of chivalry underwent something of a revival, as did English royal interest in France. The *First English Life of Henry V* (1513), largely a translation of a mid-fifteenth-century Latin life with additions from Monstrelet and from the reminiscences of an old soldier, the fourth earl of Ormonde, was dedicated to Henry VIII and begun during the latter's own war with France, so that the king

> by the knowledge and sight of this pamphile should partly be provoked in his said war to ensue the noble and chivalrous acts of this so noble, so virtuous, and so excellent prince, which so followed, he might the rather attain to like honour, fame and victory.[31]

A similar dedication and hope of emulation is found in the

preface to the second volume of Berners' translation of Froissart, and recent work on Henry VIII has suggested that he did indeed like to see himself as Henry V reborn. As Berners wrote in the prologue to his first volume – and here we have a direct echo of Froissart's own intent:

> What pleasure shall it be to the noble gentylmen of England to se, beholde, and rede the highe enterprises, famous actes and glorious dedes done and atchyved by their valiant ancestors.[32]

When we learn that Berners was captain of Calais and had been present at the siege of Tournai in 1513, and that the gentlemen of England were becoming increasingly obsessed with lineage and heraldry, then the interest in earlier high points of English successes in France is not surprising. As Morgan's recent study has shown, the claim to gentility by some of Cheshire's Tudor gentry was by virtue of their forbears' service in the French wars. Moreover, the Anglo-French wars were still being recorded in chivalric fashion, as the early sixteenth-century 'Chronicle of Calais' shows, being composed in a style similar to that of Basset and Hanson by Richard Turpyn, a serving garrison soldier whose son became a herald.[33]

As has often been shown, the Tudors purposefully denigrated their fifteenth-century royal predecessors, but when it came to Anglo-French relations, the issue was not so clear cut. After all, conflict between the two nations was still simmering and at times overt. There is thus in Tudor works little sign of criticism of those late medieval kings who pursued warlike ambitions abroad, or of English claims to French lands and titles. Edward III and Henry V are treated as much like heroes as they were in writings of their own time, not surprisingly given the derivative nature of much historical composition. Here, too, it is worth re-emphasising that many later historians used the more accessible Tudor histories interchangeably with, or even instead of, works written during the wars themselves.

The Seventeenth and Eighteenth Centuries

It is difficult to come to simple conclusions on historical writing on the wars in the two centuries or so following the death of Elizabeth I in 1603. It is all too easy to dismiss or caricature writings of these centuries in the belief that only since the late nineteenth century, with an increasingly critical and scientific approach to history, has a better informed and more accurate analysis of the Anglo-French wars emerged. In broad terms this may be true, but there are some important caveats.

Most books of the period which considered the wars were general histories of England, Britain or France. These were produced in large quantities, for history was seen as an edifying and useful element in the education of a gentleman. The full title of *The New, Impartial and Complete History of England* (London, 1790), the work of E. Barnard, Esquire, 'assisted by several gentlemen who have made the history of this country their peculiar study', shows its intention as 'to display the patriotic virtues of our illustrious ancestors and to inspire the present age with an emulation of imitating their glorious examples'. Gentlemen's libraries were full of historical works, many multi-volumed, treating of long periods and entirely derivative one from another or else based upon a selective reading of the published chronicles and Tudor histories.[34] They continued to emulate the Classical tradition in following a narrative of each reign by a judgement on the qualities of the ruler. These judgements often seem to us banal and uncritical, as well as anachronistic, written as though the rulers in question were contemporary statesmen rather than medieval kings. The essential events of the wars were well established and uncontroversial, as is also revealed in another popular genre of the time, volumes of chronological tables rather akin to modern exam cribs. A 'national' stance was also common in these centuries of frequent Anglo-French antagonism, with considerable implications for the histories of earlier conflicts. Barnard writes, for instance, that,

> to Edward III we owe the superiority which in his time the English began to obtain over the French, and which, should their councils be directed by wise and honest men, it is hoped they will maintain to the latest posterity. (p.193)

20

Inevitably, some works were better than others and some strike us as remarkably impressive for their time. This can be revealed by considering their attention to sources and by noting their attempts to come to substantiated conclusions. With respect to sources, even in the late Elizabethan period there had been attempts to make accessible government records of the past. Men like Stowe and Sir Robert Cotton (d.1631) transcribed and collected unpublished materials which were consulted by historians, all the more so when they passed to the British Museum after its founding in 1753. The sources thus preserved include many relevant to the Anglo-French wars, such as extracts from now-lost military indentures in Stowe MS 440 and, in the Cottonian collections, copies of diplomatic materials, versions of the London Chronicles and ordinances of war issued for the conquest of Maine in the 1420s.[35]

The eighteenth century saw several major advances in 'study aids'. The first was the publication of Thomas Rymer's *Foedera* (first edition 1704–13) where were printed, from manuscript sources, the major diplomatic documents of British history from the reign of Henry III to the 1650s. As the notes to this present and any other work on the subject will show, this, in its various editions, remains to the present day an essential source book. Also important was the first printing, by Thomas Hearne at Oxford in the first half of the eighteenth century, of such important chronicles as Robert of Avesbury, and several lives of Henry V. From 1767 the Rolls of Parliament from their origins in the 1330s began to appear in print at the expense of the government, although historians had already been able to draw upon a serviceable seventeenth-century abridgement. In addition, handbooks to the location of government records (then kept in many repositories in London and Westminster in a semi-haphazard state) were produced, and Carte began to publish extracts from the Gascon and Norman rolls relating to the English tenure of both areas. Similar developments occurred in France in the seventeenth and eighteenth centuries, with the collecting and publication of manuscripts, both chronicles and governmental records. In the 1760s, a Frenchman, Bréquigny, spent three years sifting through the archives housed in the Tower of London and transcribing extracts from the Norman rolls and other sources produced during the English occupation of the fifteenth century, although his work did not appear in print until the 1850s. Two further eighteenth-century French clerics are worthy of note, Dom Bévy and Dom Lenoir. It is by their transcriptions from the records of the French crown's *Chambre des Comptes* that we have, respectively, some of the accounts of the French war treasurers of the late middle ages and details of many land grants made by Henry V and Henry VI in Lancastrian Normandy. The original documents were destroyed partly by a fire in 1737 and by the destruction of documents during the French Revolution.[36]

To some degree, this collecting and editing is what we would term 'antiquarian', being done for its own sake rather than to assist in the interpretation of the past. Some of the better historians of the seventeenth and eighteenth centuries did, however, use to advantage newly published texts and unpublished manuscripts, and were imbued with enough of the notions of scholarship to footnote their work. John Speed, for instance, in his *Historie of Great Britaine* (1611) refers in his sections on the wars to several original charters which he or someone else must have consulted in one of the government's uncatalogued record repositories, and to chronicles which we know to have existed only in manuscript at the time of writing. Thomas Carte, in the second volume of his *General History of England* (1750), consciously compared the chronicles with the Rolls of Parliament and governmental records, 'without which their mistakes could not be corrected, nor the confusion that appears in their relations be redressed'. If he omitted an amusing story found in the chronicles 'which hath been adopted by modern writers to grace, embellish or enliven their performances', it was as 'a result of a careful and impartial examination of all relations and a full conviction of such stories'. This policy had apparently upset some readers of his first volume who were used to history based on Froissart, but it enabled Carte to identify, for instance, the 'irresolution and unsteadiness' which modern historians have also detected in Edward III's actions in 1339–40.[37]

There are several English and French works of this period which compare favourably with later works in terms of scholarship. Even in 1960, McKisack commended Joshua Barnes's *The History of Edward the Third* (London, 1688) as 'still on balance the best we have'.[38] Whilst Barnes praised his subject (as did Carte and most others), some were prepared to criticise. Indeed, many of the observations of modern historians about the wars can be found in works of this period, although without the level of development of argument we would now expect. David Hume's view in his *History of England* that Edward III's 'foreign wars were ... neither founded in justice nor directed to any salutary purpose' was carefully justified by his account of events. He noticed, for instance, the weakness of support in France and the likelihood that, with such feeble beginnings, the war might have ended in 1341 had not the Breton war of succession occurred. Hume, a Scotsman, also emphasised the excessive costs of Edward's wars. Later in the century, Robert Henry, also Scottish, suggested in his *History of Great Britain* that Edward might never have prosecuted his claim had it not been for French support for the Scots. Rapin de Thoyras' *History of England* (1732), the work of a Huguenot expelled from France and carefully based upon Rymer's *Foedera*, even warned against exaggerating Henry V's achievements, suggesting that he was motivated by avarice and gross ambition. He considered that Edward III deserved more praise in his French wars for he had to deal with a united France whereas Henry was able to take advantage of internal divisions.[39] Thus whilst many works slavishly follow the well-worn lines of Tudor and earlier versions, some works deal critically but fairly with the Anglo-French wars, often without the excessive prejudices of many nineteenth-century works. It is also interesting to see how well known in this period French works were in England and how much historians drew upon works in both languages.

The Nineteenth Century

As we move into the nineteenth century, various influences on historical treatment of the wars can be detected. First, the collection and publication of materials continued, but now more systematically, under the aegis of governments and newly-formed historical societies. From 1857 the Rolls Series in England published new editions of chronicles, including those of Avesbury, Murimuth, Waurin, Blondel and Berry, as well as an important compilation of material concerning the fifteenth-century wars. The first scholarly edition of Froissart was produced by Kervyn de Lettenhove at Brussels between 1867 and 1877, with a final supplementary volume providing relevant material from contemporary record evidence. The Société de l'Histoire de France (1833) and regional societies such as the Société de l'Histoire de Normandie (1870) put into print much late medieval material. In both France and England care for national records was improved. The Public Record Office was founded in 1838 and records gradually moved to it from their dispersed repositories, but it was not until the end of the century that good cataloguing permitted easy consultation.

Secondly, intellectual trends in Europe around 1800 had a marked effect upon how the wars were considered. The Romantic movement stimulated a rather anachronistic interest in all things medieval, but some aspects of the later middle ages, such as the chivalry and drama of warfare, suited Romantic interpretations particularly well. It is not surprising, then, that Sir Walter Scott should himself toy with, although never begin, editing Froissart, declaring him to be 'the most entertaining, and perhaps the most valuable historian of the Middle Ages'.[40] Scott can be credited with the invention of the term 'War of the Roses' for the English domestic conflicts which followed the defeats of 1450–3, and the approach he favoured is reflected in the more orthodox world of historical writing by Hallam's *State of Europe* and by much popular historical writing in nineteenth-century England and France. Balzac went so far as to lament that the History of France had been 'Walter Scottée', and indeed many historical works of this century suggest that the writing of history had been brought as close to that of literature as it was in the time of the wars themselves.[41] It was perhaps under the influence of this 'Romantic' view that the term 'Hundred Years War' emerged in 1861 and was taken up so avidly.

By the later nineteenth century two conflicting trends in

historical writing on the wars can be identified. At the same time as attention to sources and the professional study of history advanced, so too did the mass market as the level of literacy reached unparalleled heights. These trends coexisted uneasily, leading even reputable historians to certain excesses. J. R. Green's influential *History of the English People* (London, 1878) follows twenty-two pages on the history of England from 1327 to 1346 with seven pages on the battle of Crécy based entirely upon the chronicles, and then gives up six pages of the eighteen discussing the period 1422 to 1453 to Joan of Arc. This unbalanced, dramatic and jingoistic approach coloured many school textbooks and popular works well into the twentieth century.

The mention of jingoism brings us to a further element in the change of attitudes between the eighteenth and nineteenth centuries. The French Revolution and the Napoleonic wars fundamentally affected English attitudes to France. The wars confirmed the need to mistrust the French, just as victory in them strengthened the notion of English superiority. Throughout the nineteenth century, the English were worried by continuing political instability in France, and in the 1850s spent thousands on defending their country in fear of French invasion. The close ties with French civilisation which had existed earlier were loosened. The editors of the Rolls Series, for instance, considered it necessary to translate French chronicles into English for the benefit of readers, but assumed that all would be able to understand medieval Latin. Historians, like most of the population, became convinced of their Germanic rather than their French connections, and were increasingly obsessed with constitutional history. The result for the historiography of the wars was declining interest and increasing criticism, but based on contemporary prejudices rather than on study of the sources. As McKisack puts it so well, 'Like the smoke rising from the factory chimneys, the mists of a doctrinaire liberalism rose between historians and the heroes of the past'. As she shows in her study of writings on Edward III, his reputation declined to a particularly low ebb in the works of Lingard (1854), Stubbs (1866), Tout (1905) and Ramsey (1913), and even the generally eulogistic Longman (1869) urged his readers not to be dazzled by his victories.[42] The wars were seen as lacking in constitutional significance and their cost offended contemporary notions of goodhousekeeping of the nation's finances. Henry V fared a little better, as Allmand's outline of the historiography of the reign shows, but even he was not entirely immune from criticism.[43]

The Twentieth Century

Except for works aimed at the popular market, the Hundred Years War was treated rather unsympathetically in late nineteenth- and early twentieth-century historical writing in England. Until the end of the Second World War, it was mainly left to the French and the Americans to apply the new, rigorously source-based methodology to in-depth analysis of particular themes and issues. When the American Cuttino reviewed the modern historiography of the Hundred Years War in 1956 he suggested that the point of departure should be taken as Gavrilovitch's *Etude sur le Traité de Paris de 1259* (Paris, 1899).[44] Before 1899, the wars had been treated mainly in general histories of France and England. Gavrilovitch's work typified the high level of attention now being paid to governmental records as opposed to chronicle evidence, and represented a new approach influenced by the contemporary scene – the study of international relations through diplomacy. It also stressed the growing, although not completely novel, view that the treaty of 1259, when the English king surrendered his claim to Normandy, Anjou and Maine and agreed to pay liege homage to the French king for an enlarged Gascony, was the crucial turning point in Anglo-French relations, and the real origin of the Hundred Years War.

Three years later, Déprez published *Les Préliminaires de la Guerre de Cent Ans. La Papauté, la France et l'Angleterre, 1328– 1342* (Paris, 1902) in an attempt to fill what he saw as the main lacuna in the study of the war, its diplomatic history. His book drew not only on French and English records but also on those of the papacy, which was so closely involved in negotiations before and after the outbreak of war in 1337. Déprez' conclusion followed the same line as that of Gavrilovitch, arguing that since 1259 the French kings had consistently tried to exploit their feudal superiority over the English king/dukes in the hope of removing them by judicial process. In Edward III, Philip VI was faced with an English monarch who refused to accept or to discuss the judicial position, and who was prepared to go to war with his feudal overlord, disguising his real ambitions (for Gascony in full sovereignty) by a claim to the French throne. For Déprez, then, the claim to the throne was a means to an end, not an end in itself – a way of encouraging support for a war which in its feudal guise had not raised much enthusiasm in England, of intimidating the king of France, and of demanding territorial compensation in return for surrendering the claim to the throne.

The stress on diplomacy and on the thirteenth-century feudal origins of the war has dominated much twentieth-century writing on the war, as is more fully described in Cuttino's review of the historiography in 1956 and Vale's up-date of 1989.[45] There has been considerable interest in the period from 1259 to 1337, as is evident in Cuttino's own study of *English Diplomatic Administration, 1259–1339* (1940), which gives much space to the various attempts of negotiators to resolve the judicial problem of Aquitaine, and in the writings of Pierre Chaplais on the status of the duchy and on the intricacies of diplomacy. Whilst the issue of Gascony has loomed large in all works, including the principal modern narrative history of the Hundred Years War by Perroy (1945), there have been slight variations of emphasis. For Tout (1930), Wolffe (1953), Cuttino (1956) and Chaplais (1948 and 1963), for instance, the dispute over sovereignty was insoluble because it lay between rulers who were expanding their authority as kings, thus making it impossible, and anachronistic, for one to be the vassal of the other. Templeman (1952), however, saw the matter as a property dispute, arguing that modern notions of sovereignty were not applicable. He also argued that, whilst Gascony was a major issue, Edward III's problems in Scotland were also an important catalyst to war in 1337, as were the personalities of Edward, Philip VI and Pope

Benedict XII.[46] Wolffe (1953) began the move away from an exclusively diplomatic approach, suggesting that the attitude of the Gascons themselves formed the major stumbling block to an amicable settlement between the French and English kings. Vale's recent work on the duchy has explored this more fully, leading him to the conclusion that 1294, when Philip IV's confiscation of Aquitaine led to the first Anglo-French war since the 1240s, was a more important turning point than 1259.[47] Others, such as Colville (1940–1) and Lewis (1980), have suggested that Anglo-French hostility goes back to the Norman invasion of 1066, or in the eyes of Templeman and Le Patourel (1965), to 1204 when Normandy was lost, so that the Hundred Years War was an attempt to revive the Angevin Empire.[48] In general, modern historians have been eager to extend the Hundred Years War backwards in time, and thus perhaps to diminish its status as a major point of departure in medieval European history, looking instead at long-term changes from the thirteenth century onwards. There has been more of a reluctance to go forwards, perhaps because this would be treading on the toes of early modernists who have already decided that French involvement in Italy and the rise of religious conflict were of greater significance than the continuance of Anglo-French hostility.

In both English and French studies of the war, the territorial dimension has been seen as the main cause of the origin and continuation of Anglo-French conflict in the later middle ages. In fact there is now no really perceptible difference between approaches and opinions in the two countries. The experiences of fighting on the same side in two world wars and of growing European integration have gradually brought the nations and their historians together, although Tout's *France and England: their relations in the Middle Ages and Now* (Manchester, 1922) reminds us of just how fragile relations still were in the 1920s. It is today realised that the two kingdoms must be studied in tandem. For instance, historians now generally agree that the wars were not *caused* by a sense of nationalism but that they *generated* such feeling. The researches of Rowe, Allmand, Massey, Thompson and others have reminded us that English rulers acted as legitimate French kings in the parts of northern France which they occupied in the fifteenth century. Such policies cannot be understood unless the historian has a good knowledge of the system of French royal government which already existed.[49]

The claim to the throne, which before the end of the nineteenth century was taken at face value, has been dismissed; John Le Patourel (1958) stands as a voice in the wilderness in suggesting

> that Edward's claim to the throne of France was meant more seriously and deserves to be taken more seriously than it has been by historians during the present century, both as to its merits and as to its place in his war aims.

The modern stance has been to consider Henry V's claim too as truly reflective of his intentions only from October 1419, and to argue that on his death-bed he envisaged the possibility that the title might be surrendered in return for full sovereignty in Normandy.[50] The dismissal of the claim to the throne by historians is perhaps a reflection of the concerns of our century, when international legal disputes over landownership and territorial sovereignty are still familiar but where notions of royal authority are much diminished.

Several further trends in twentieth-century historical research on the wars can be identified, all of which have encouraged a move away from the reign-based approach which dominated much of the earlier historical writing. The first is the study of the administration of war, which stems from the interest in constitutional history in the late nineteenth century. The wars have been set in the context of developments in the study of royal government, such as in Tout's *Chapters in English Administrative History* (1920–33), and of parliament and war taxation, as for instance in the works of Harriss. American historians, most notably Newhall and Prince, carried out detailed examinations of military bureaucracy, although there is as yet no English parallel to Contamine's detailed study of the armies of the French kings in the fourteenth and fifteenth centuries.

The second trend is the examination of the socio-economic

aspects of war, much influenced by such concerns in this century and by the leanings of historians of the Marxist persuasion and of the French *Annales* school. The stress which French chroniclers placed upon the damaging effects of repeated English invasions (after all, most of the Hundred Years War took place in France) was echoed in Deniflé's highly influential work of 1897–9, *La Désolation des églises, monastères et hopitaux en France pendant la Guerre de Cent Ans*. It has been given further emphasis by more recent regional studies. Guy Bois' (1976) coining of the term 'Hiroshima en Normandie' to describe the economic conditions of the duchy under Lancastrian rule stands out as the most extreme statement ever on this theme. It is interesting to note that the first real consideration of the 'costs' of the war for England was published by Postan in 1942, at a time when 'the present war' was, in the author's eyes, 'bound to transform the entire economy of the world'. The debate which he initiated still rumbles on.[51]

The third trend, determined by the nature of doctorate research in British and French universities particularly since the Second World War, is to approach the subject through the study of a particular area or person. This has led to the publication of some highly illuminating regional studies and biographies. Recent research, sometimes unpublished, can be pieced together to provide a fuller picture of the wars and their context. 'Context' is perhaps the key word for modern historians. As Allmand writes in the most recent general study of the Hundred Years War,

> What the historian is trying to do is not merely to record the events and happenings of war, but to study them against the background of the world in which the long Anglo-French conflict was fought.[52]

His book considers the wars from more angles than any previous work because it has been made clear by modern researches that they impinged on so much. Their study is no longer merely a recitation of battles or heroes. The investigation of what the French call *mentalité* has become as important as that of events. The use of the term 'Hundred Years War' has perhaps proved useful in encouraging us to take a longer and more comparative perspective.

There are essentially two ways, perhaps, in which modern historical work on the wars differs from that of the past. First, detailed investigation has shown just how complicated international relations, military activities and political machinations were. By contrast older works seem remarkably thin and straightforward, for our increased knowledge has made us so much less ready to be categoric. The second difference is that modern historians consult as many sources as possible. But as with their forebears they are still at the mercy of their sources. Vast quantities of late medieval governmental records survive in France and England; in fact one recent French commentator has gone so far as to suggest that the English lost Normandy in the mid-fifteenth century because they were over-bureaucratic.[53] Yet rulers did not keep separate archives for their wars or for international relations – another good reason why these topics must be seen in the wider context of late medieval government. Evidence of military expenditure, for instance, must be gleaned from the standard records of the English Exchequer or the French *Chambre des Comptes*, diplomatic activity from a variety of sources: Rymer did not print it all. The records are incomplete, which is not surprising given the vicissitudes they have suffered in the five or six centuries since their production. French sources were much dispersed and destroyed before and during the Revolution. The English left behind most of the records of their fifteenth-century occupation of Normandy, and these are now to be found in at least nine record repositories worldwide. The historian of the Hundred Years War, then, still has a good deal of detective work to do, and some topics remain in need of detailed study. There is at least another hundred years' research to do on what, as McFarlane aptly remarked, 'we have agreed to miscall the Hundred Years War'.[54]

2

ORIGINS AND OBJECTIVES: ANGLO-FRENCH CONFLICT IN THE FOURTEENTH CENTURY

Feudal Origins

In 1337, Edward III held the county of Ponthieu, straddling the Somme. He also bore the title duke of Aquitaine, although the territory he actually held in south-west France was little more than a 50-mile-wide coastal strip between Bayonne and Bordeaux. This was a far cry from the days of Henry II when a king of England held the whole of western France: from the duchy of Normandy in the north, through the counties of Anjou, Maine, Touraine and Poitou to the extensive duchy of Aquitaine in the south, with additional claims to the overlordship of the duchy of Brittany and county of Flanders. Much happened between the twelfth and early fourteenth centuries, but in many ways, the two basic issues of English royal lands in France remained the same: the relationship between the kings of England and France which their tenure generated, and their rightful extent. It was impossible to find a peaceful solution to Anglo-French differences in 1337 because the issues had been so long-running, and had repeatedly proved themselves incapable of lasting settlement. The reasons for this, however, need to be seen in the context of each successive conflict as well as in the problems inherent in the issues themselves. A further major stumbling block was that the dispute was between kings, and was thus much affected by wider considerations of international relations and domestic politics. As a result, the issues were always more than 'little local difficulties', often assuming Europe-wide dimensions, as is more fully explored in chapter 4.

That the lands were held of the king of France was difficult, if not impossible, to deny, even in the second half of the twelfth century when the English king ruled more of France than the French king himself. After all, both the Norman and Angevin dynasties in England stemmed from ducal and comital roots in France: both had thus accepted their obligation to pay some kind of homage to the French king for their lands in France.[1] The fact that they were not sovereign in their continental lands mattered little whilst the French monarchy was weak and they were strong. Over the second half of the twelfth century, however, the French monarchy developed its power largely by exploiting its feudal rights to the limit. Here it was helped by the internecine struggles within the Angevin family. Thus in the treaty of Le Goulet (May 1200) King John was prepared to pay homage to Philip II along with an almost unprecedented relief of 20,000 marks in order to be confirmed as holder of all the Angevin lands in France. More importantly, the treaty made clear Philip's right as overlord to interfere in John's government of his fiefs by forcing him to pardon the rebellious barons of Angoulême and Limoges.[2]

There were, during the next 137 years, difficulties over the notion of one king paying homage to another, not least because this implied an obligation to provide military service against the French king's enemies. If the latter were the English king's allies, there was a considerable danger that the possession of non-sovereign lands in France could impede English foreign policy. But the greatest problem was undoubtedly the French king's right as overlord to interfere in a vassal's government of his own fief. In particular the French king could hear appeals which the subjects of a vassal might make against their lord. In 1201 the Lusignan brothers, barons in Poitou, appealed to Philip against John. Philip followed feudal custom by summoning John to his court to answer the charges, and, when he failed to appear, by confiscating his fiefs in April 1202.[3] In the wars which ensued, John lost all his possessions in the north, Normandy, Maine, Anjou and Touraine, holding at his death only the Channel Islands, most of Poitou and the duchy of Aquitaine. Poitou was lost in 1224.

This right of the French king to hear appeals remained crucial, with a second, more general, element developing alongside – the question of precisely what jurisdiction the overlord possessed in his vassals' fiefs. Could royal officials, for instance, exercise their authority therein, collect taxes, summon the vassal's subjects to the royal courts? As the theory and practice of government developed over the thirteenth century, these conflicts of jurisdiction were bound to increase. None of this was unique to the relationship of the French king and his English royal vassal. French kings applied the same degree of interference elsewhere, most notably in their dealings with the counts of Flanders. But the kingly status of the English royal vassals presented unique problems. Although they technically held Aquitaine as dukes, their policies there could not fail to be affected by their policies as kings of England. As royal administration developed in England, so too did the king/dukes seek to expand their control in Aquitaine. At the same time the kings of France were seeking to extend their authority over the whole of France. It was not easy for the English kings to separate their notions of royal and of ducal sovereignty. Indeed it was all the more difficult once the loss of most of the northern French lands had shifted the political centre to England. What was left in their hands – the duchy of Aquitaine – had been, after all, the most distant, least valuable and initially least integrated of all the Angevin lands. The lands of the 'Angevin Empire' had been held together before 1204 by the fact they were all held by the same person, who just happened to be king of England as well. Over the course of the reign of Henry III the nature of the remaining continental landholdings changed. When in 1254 he bestowed the revenues of the duchy on his eldest son, the lord Edward (later Edward I), he did so 'in such a manner that they may never be separated from the crown but should remain to the king of England forever'.[4] By this date, if not earlier, the duchy was seen as an inalienable part of the English crown, although still technically possessed and ruled by the king as duke of Aquitaine.

Aquitaine was never an easy area to govern. Its semi-independent and frequently feuding nobility had caused problems even for earlier dukes. It had complicated tenurial patterns, a lack of the sort of feudalism common to the other Angevin territories of England, Normandy and Anjou, and a stress on Roman rather than customary law, and throughout its tenure by English kings its rule remained an exercise in persuasion. Relations between the king/duke and the Gascon nobility formed a crucial element in Anglo-French animosity. Some nobles held of both kings and could exploit the conflict to their own ends; some wavered in their loyalty, and could be persuaded by the French king's officials to appeal against their lord; others remained loyal to the English king despite French pressure and personal losses.[5]

In administration and economy, the duchy after 1204 has been said to resemble a colony.[6] Its chief officers – the seneschal responsible for judicial and administrative matters, and the constable of Bordeaux for finances – were rarely natives. Many matters concerning its government were handled in London. It had a small English settlement; it was, like Ireland, a land of opportunity – a sort of medieval Wild West – where there was still potential for making money and gaining status. This explains the bastides (fortified towns and villages) which sprang up during the thirteenth century, often at the initiative of settlers and administrators although also with the involvement of local seigneurs, for economic as well as military purposes. Gascony was an important market for English cloth, leather and grain, and provided the main source of England's wine, with the crown collecting custom on wine both in the duchy and in England. The duchy was worth around £13,000 per annum to the crown in 1324. But one ought not to place too much store by financial concerns. English kings did not wish to hold on to the duchy because it brought them revenue but because it was hereditarily theirs.

Indeed, there are strong arguments against a colonial analogy. The duchy retained its own legal system. The Gascons were not second-class citizens, but were often highly privileged because the lack of a large English garrison or settlement made their military support crucial; the defence of the duchy was largely manned and financed by the natives themselves. The duchy was never completely run from England, and some Gascons found their way into administrative service in England. In some ways it resembled an English county, having most in common, perhaps, with the (from 1238 royal) palatinate of Chester, with its own institutions, representative body, and tax systems, its particular liberties and its inalienability from the English crown. 'Liberties' and 'inalienability' were much stressed by the Gascons. As with the palatinate of Chester, some of the peculiarities of Gascony existed before royal takeover, others were introduced under royal rule because of the distinctive relationship with the crown. In Chester, however, the English king had no feudal superior: in Aquitaine he did. That was a crucial difference.

To return to the relationship with the king of France, after 1202 the French kings still regarded the Angevin inheritance as confiscated and thus addressed John and Henry III only as kings of England and lords of Ireland. Although the appeal had come in 1201 from Poitou, Philip had cleverly summoned John in all his titles, and was thus able to consider all the latter's possessions confiscated. The northern lands were kept in royal hands. In 1241 Poitou was vested in Alphonso, Louis IX's brother, to be held of the French crown. In 1242, southern Saintonge, the most north-westerly part of Aquitaine, fell to the French and was added to Alphonso's appanage. Two years later Henry III abandoned military efforts to recover the lost lands yet still clung to all the titles which his father had held.

The reasons why a negotiated settlement was reached between Henry III and Louis IX on 13 October 1259 are complex, and cannot be fully investigated here. The terms of this Treaty of Paris, however, need elucidation, because they have often been seen as sowing the seeds of the Hundred Years War.[7] In the treaty Henry III agreed to surrender his claim and titles to Normandy, Anjou, Maine, Touraine and Poitou. Until the Hundred Years War, this clause was not reneged upon by English kings in any of their subsequent disputes with the

French. In return, the treaty confirmed Henry's possession of Aquitaine and made territorial concessions to bring it to almost the extent held in 1204. Much had happened in the areas since they had been lost, so that not all of the conceded lands could be handed over immediately. Acquisition of the Agenais, Quercy and Saintonge depended upon Alphonso and his wife dying childless. As a result, the clauses concerning these areas were very complicated (envisaging the possibility of financial compensation instead of territorial acquisition) and were thus responsible for much future Anglo-French controversy. Even what was transferred immediately was not without its problems. Louis IX gave Henry 'all the right that he has and holds' in the bishoprics and cities of Limoges, Cahors and Périgueux, except for 'those things which he [Louis] cannot alienate owing to letters granted by him or his successors'. There were many here known as *privilegiati* who held inalienably of the French king, and whose acceptance of the English king was by no means assured.[8] It is unlikely, however, that Louis IX had deliberately made the transfer clauses complex. At this stage in his life, Louis seems to have been genuinely dedicated to Anglo-French peace, but he could not deny the rights of existing landholders. Potentially, too, Henry had much to gain as the chances of Alphonso and Joan having children seemed remote.

By the treaty, Henry promised to do liege homage to Louis IX for any lands which came into his possession by its terms, and also for Bordeaux, Bayonne and for Gascony 'and for all the land that we hold beyond the English Channel in fief and domain ... and we will hold of him as a peer of France and as duke of Aquitaine'. The significance of this clause has been much debated, again because it was to prove a bone of contention later on. At first sight it seems to mark no real departure from the situation under the Angevins when homage had been paid for lands held of the French crown. The two crucial words, however, were 'liege' and 'Gascony'. The form of homage had never before been defined as liege, which implied a personal subservience. But we should beware of reading too much into the introduction of the term. It is possible that Henry and Louis envisaged the homage to be the same as that paid before 1202, and that they felt that 'liege' was the appropriate and precedented form. Certainly Henry had no objections to paying such homage to Louis soon after the treaty was sealed. An alternative interpretation is that Louis wanted a stronger form of homage for his own ends, and that Henry, faced with growing political difficulties at home and thus desperately in need of the 500 knights which Louis was prepared to finance, had little choice but to agree.

This interpretation can also be applied to the specific mention of Gascony. It is possible that the Angevins and their predecessors as dukes had never paid homage for Gascony (technically only the extreme south-western part of Aquitaine, but often applied to a wider area) because it was not a fief but an allod, and thus held freely without the need for homage to the French crown. If this was the case, then Louis was again acting in his own interests when he included Gascony in the territories for which liege homage was to be performed. A major problem in interpreting the treaty is that the earlier status and geographical extent of Gascony remains ambiguous. Certainly the treaty made no mention of any change from allod to fief. The English did not bring up the allod argument until 1298. By then, four years of open war had prompted Edward I to seek whatever means he could to overturn or modify the Treaty of Paris.

Did the Treaty of Paris damage the position of the king/duke? Writing 60 years later, Joinvill claimed that many of Louis IX's barons opposed the settlement because it gave too much to Henry III. Louis justified himself thus: 'it seems to me that what I have given him I have used well, because he was not my man, but by it he has entered into my homage.' This has been taken to relate both to the supposed innovation of liege homage and to the inclusion of the Gascon 'allod', but it could be interpreted in a more general sense.[9] After all, no homage had been paid since 1200, for the lands were still technically confiscate and the kings still at war. Yet English kings had remained in the meantime in *de facto* possession of much of the duchy of Aquitaine. In 1259 Henry unequivocally became Louis' vassal: Louis supported Henry against his rebellious barons in England, and the treaty preserved peace between the kings for the rest of their lives.

Some care needs to be exercised when dealing with the reign

of Edward I. Whilst Edward may have objected to his father's treaty he was bound by it, and until 1294 his aim seems to have been to implement it. Homage was renewable at any change of king on either side of the Channel; thus Edward paid it on 6 August 1273 to Philip III. Much has been made of the words he used: 'for the lands that I *ought* to hold of you.' This was a clear allusion to the fact that, although Alphonso of Poitiers had died in 1271 and his lands had escheated to the French crown, the Agenais and Saintonge had not yet been transferred to the English king. Yet Edward's words and subsequent actions were not tantamount to a rejection of the treaty. In 1279 his wife, Eleanor of Castile, inherited the county of Ponthieu from her mother; an amicable arrangement was made with the French king in the Treaty of Amiens (May 1279). Edward agreed to pay liege homage for the county, as was entirely appropriate, plus a relief of 6000 *livres parisis,* and Philip III promised to hold the enquiry into Quercy which the Treaty of Paris had envisaged.[10] By 9 August 1279, the Agenais had been transferred and Edward had acknowledged that he held it in liege homage. After Philip IV came to the throne Edward again paid liege homage (October 1285): 'I become your man for the lands which I hold from you on this side of the sea according to the form of peace made between our ancestors.' This became standard terminology thenceforward and was apparently taken by Edward in 1298 as meaning that homage was conditional upon the full implementation of the Treaty of Paris. It could be seen as implying, however, that the form of homage was merely as envisaged in that treaty. In 1280 it was agreed that Quercy should be held by the English king in exchange for the lands and rights in the three dioceses, and that Saintonge should be handed over; it was effectively annexed to Gascony three years later.[11]

The territorial clauses of the Treaty of Paris had therefore been implemented, although there remained many boundary and jurisdictional disputes. When war broke out in 1294 it was not over any issue mentioned in the treaty. It arose from the clash of advancing royal administrations, and from circumstances within the duchy itself, as the studies by Vale have revealed. War came essentially over appeals, as it had done in

1202. The treaty said nothing about the mechanisms of appeal but legitimised them implicitly through the payment of homage. Since the treaty, although not so much due to it *per se* as to the fact that it had restored diplomatic relations between the duke and his royal overlord, the number of appeals had increased. Within the duchy society was as fractious as ever and in the newly-acquired areas, including Ponthieu, there were even more causes for dispute. Behind all this lay the expansion of French royal interest in matters judicial, as witnessed by the development of the Paris *parlement* as a supreme court in the late thirteenth century. Even worse, whilst an appeal was *sub judice*, the petitioner could fly the French flag and ignore ducal officials. Edward I, a stickler for his own prerogatives, sought to staunch the flow of appeals, because it diminished both his own and his officials' authority in the duchy, and potentially undermined his relationship with the French king. The problem of appeals was thus discussed when homage was paid in 1285; a compromise was reached by Philip IV agreeing to a three-month moratorium after an appeal was presented to allow the duke's administration opportunity to settle the affair. From 1286 to 1289, Edward I was resident in the duchy (the last ever visit of an English king), attempting to streamline its administration and judicial systems to prevent clashes of jurisdiction and grounds for appeal.[12]

Like Edward III's wars, the outbreak of hostilities in 1294 had as much to do with European politics as with local difficulties. Vale points in particular to the role of Aragon both in the failure of the French 'crusade' of 1285 and in the on-going struggle with the Capetian dukes of Anjou over Sicily. Anglo-French relations deteriorated considerably in the early 1290s. Unprecedented numbers of appellants from Aquitaine were seen in Paris. The reforms made by Edward during his visit seem to have exacerbated rather than mitigated jurisdictional conflicts, and in his actions we can detect perhaps more of a 'colonial' attitude to the duchy than ever before. In addition, the Capetians were encouraging, possibly even bribing, men to bring appeals, not only in Aquitaine but also in Flanders, whose count was also seen to be too independent. On 27 October 1293 Philip IV summoned Edward to his court to answer complaints which had been made against his ducal officials in Aquitaine. Edward did not turn up, but his subsequent actions show that he was quite prepared to negotiate.[13] It is difficult to see the war which ensued from the confiscation of the duchy in May 1294 as occasioned by anything other than French aggression, in which the French exploited many spurious appeals as well as the recent flare-up of clashes at sea between Gascon and Norman sailors, and a supposed Gascon raid on the French-held town of La Rochelle. The French were certainly more prepared for war than Edward was, as is witnessed by the ease with which their troops took virtually all the English-held lands in Ponthieu and Aquitaine. It seems clear that outright conquest was the aim – the removal once and for all of the Angevins from France. We have come a long way from Louis IX's peace – and the road travelled is very much that of the development of both French and English kingship in the last quarter of the thirteenth century.

The French did not succeed in their war objectives, but it was distractions elsewhere, in Flanders and with the pope, which prevented them, rather than English ability to cling onto a coastal strip and to recover Bordeaux. The weakness of his Gascon position had forced Edward to seek allies in the Low Countries and Germany to keep up any semblance of a military threat. His position had been further undermined by the Franco-Scottish alliance of 1295. As Vale puts it, 'if the Anglo-French war of 1294–8 had proved anything it was that neither side could hope to emerge victorious from a conflict fought exclusively in Aquitaine'.[14] A settlement was equally hard to arrange now that the French had made their intentions clear. Anglo-French relations had been irreparably damaged. From 1297 distractions on both sides had forced an uneasy truce, but all that could be negotiated in the next year was a marriage between Edward and Philip's sister, intended, as many such marriages were in the middle ages, as a way of bringing the two sides closer together. Edward's stance in 1298 was significantly more hard-line than it had ever been. He then argued that Gascony was still an allod and that Edward thus had full rights of sovereignty and *ressort* (supreme justice) therein. He added that the French king was mistaken in thinking that the Treaty of Paris had converted it into a fief since no treaty could do this, adding that the French had broken the treaty by not fulfilling all the clauses concerning land transfer.[15]

When a full peace came in May 1303 (also called the Treaty of Paris) it did little more than re-establish the pre-war status quo, by restoring all the captured lands to Edward in return for the payment of liege homage.[16] Perhaps the greatest hope of reconciliation lay in the intended marriage of Philip's daughter, Isabella, to Edward's eldest son, the union from which Edward III's claim to the French throne was subsequently to derive. We can see, however, that Anglo-French relations remained strained. The issue of homage was now even more controversial as it gave retrospective justification to Philip's aggression. Thus Edward I never paid liege homage again in person, and the issue was fudged by the granting of the duchy in 1306 to his son Prince Edward (later Edward II), who could pay homage without demeaning himself. Moreover, there was no successful outcome to subsequent discussions on French support for the Scots and English aid to the Flemish. These were issues which were now as important to both kings as the question of Gascony, for Philip had suffered ignominious defeat at the hands of the Flemish at Courtrai in 1302 and the English were still at war with the Scots. These matters were never fully settled and so played a significant role in the causes of the Hundred Years War. Although Edward's lands and those of his Gascon supporters were supposed to be restored in their entirety, the war had generated many conflicting claims in the duchy which still needed settling at the time of Edward's death in 1307.

Although Edward II paid homage on his marriage to Isabella in 1308, this was not explicitly liege. The issues raised in his father's reign persisted and worsened. The question of homage was kept to the fore by three changes of French king between 1316 and 1322. Only in 1320 was homage paid, and then again it was not explicitly liege. On the other occasions excuses were made. French kings continued to receive appeals and to claim that the actions of ducal officials were undermining royal authority. Conferences on these matters held at Montreuil in

1306 and Périgueux in 1311 brought no solution. Here we can see, perhaps, the development of 'national' stances. In France, kings were claiming the rule of all their subjects, even those in the lordship of others. In 1314, for instance, Philip IV banned minting in Bordeaux unless it had royal as well as ducal licence. (It is worth remembering that since the tenth century, only the king had the right to mint in England. Thus the French kings had much ground to make up, and having vassals like the English king did not help!) In the same year the English parliament debated ways to oppose demands for homage.[17] The English could not deny that homage had been paid, but they could revive the argument that Gascony was an allod, whilst also attempting to strengthen their position with claims of the non-fulfilment of both the 1259 and 1303 treaties. A considerable amount of documentation can be shown to have been compiled in the reign of Edward II for these purposes.[18] A dispute between lord and vassal over jurisdiction and appeals had become a full international dispute between two increasingly powerful monarchies, as perhaps it had always threatened to be.

It was not surprising that war should erupt again in 1324. The French, now ruled by Charles IV, remained the aggressors, intent upon conquest or at least upon undermining the English position to make it untenable. The *casus belli* seems again to have been a trumped-up charge – the attack by the seneschal of Gascony on a provocatively-built French bastide at Saint-Sardos in the Agenais on 15 October 1323. Again too the duchy was declared confiscate (January 1324) because the king/duke refused to appear to answer charges made against his officials. The French overran Ponthieu, the Agenais and further territory in the south. In May 1325, however, they appeared to be willing to come to a settlement: the conquered lands were to be restored to Edward II's son, who was to be created duke, as his father had been in 1306, and thus pay homage and a relief of 60,000 *livres parisis*.[19] These conditions were fulfilled when Prince Edward paid homage to Charles IV at Paris on 24 September 1325, but conflict began again when the French king demanded the retention of the Agenais as a war indemnity. By 1327 he may have been envisaging an all-out invasion of the remaining

English lands.[20] When Edward II was deposed in favour of his son on 13 January 1327, the English and French were still at war. The English were now in their weakest position ever, with the need for homage by a king/duke again at issue.

Dynastic origins

Although we tend to see the death of Charles IV as crucial, the deposition of Edward II is of equal importance in understanding Anglo-French relations over the next decade. When Edward III came to the throne, he found himself at war with both the French and the Scots. The circumstances of the deposition and his age – 14 – meant that policy was controlled by his mother and Roger Mortimer, earl of March. Given their relative weakness at home, it is not surprising to find them pursuing a 'peace at all costs' policy. In their settlements with the French (Paris, 31 March 1327) and with the Scots (Northampton, 4 May 1328), English interests were sacrificed for the sake of the stability of the new regime. In the midst of all this, on 1 February 1328, Charles IV, last of the direct line of Capetian kings of France, died. The English response to this can only be understood in the light of these other events.

Isabella and Mortimer made a hasty and disadvantageous peace with the French. This was based on the settlement negotiated in 1325 but involved an additional indemnity of 50,000 marks.[21] The French did not return all of the lands they had conquered. As in the settlements of 1259 and 1303 the restitution of territory proved difficult to effect, particularly because of the resistance of French local officials. Edward III thus began his reign with less land in Aquitaine than his father had held. Moreover, all the old issues persisted. The obligation to pay homage had been accepted in the 1327 settlement, but had not been fulfilled before Charles IV died.

To understand the events of 1328 we must look back to the death of Louis X on 5 June 1316. To that point the Capetians had been blessed with a continuous line of male heirs since the late tenth century. Even now there was no cause for alarm:

Louis' pregnant widow was delivered of a son, John I, on 13 November 1316. The dilemma came when John died five days later. Louis had a daugher, Jeanne, by his first marriage, but she was only seven years old and her mother had been divorced for supposed adultery. He also had two younger brothers, of whom the eldest, Philip, count of Poitiers, had acted as Regent during the gestation and brief reign of John I. Philip had enough support and was in the right position to seize the throne and be crowned as Philip V at Reims on 9 January 1317, outmanoeuvring Jeanne's supporters. But could a woman have succeeded to the throne of France? There was no precedent, but no outright ban either, because the problem had never arisen before. None the less, Philip thought it wise to have her exclusion justified. The assembly which he summoned, meeting on 2 February, decided that women could not succeed, an unsurprising decision given that Philip had already been crowned. Jeanne had a claim to the county of Champagne and kingdom of Navarre, which were definitely hereditable by a female and indeed had come to the French crown through the wife of Philip IV. Philip accepted the validity of this claim but retained these lands in his own hands for the time being.

A woman had been passed over in the French royal succession. It was uncontroversial, therefore, that at Philip's own death on 2 January 1322, leaving only five girls, he should be succeeded by his last surviving brother (Charles IV), with his daughters being promised compensation in lieu of their territorial rights. Whilst the crown could not pass to a woman, tenurial custom allowed heiresses a share of family lands, although kings made every effort to maintain the royal demesne intact. Like Louis X, Charles IV died leaving a daughter and a pregnant third wife. This time a girl was born (1 April 1328), but again the Regent, this time Charles's cousin, Philip count of Valois, took the throne. Subsequently, Philip (VI) effected compensation for the territorial rights of his various nieces, and allowed Jeanne, now married to Philip, count of Evreux, to succeed to the kingdom of Navarre.

In France Philip was the obvious heir. He was aged 35 and already had a son to succeed him. He had been approved, perhaps even 'elected' by an assembly of notables which, as Regent, he had summoned on 2 April 1328. As far as we know, no claim was put forward on behalf of any of his nieces. But there was one difference from the situation in 1317. Philip was not the only male with a claim to the throne. The other was Edward III, nephew of Charles IV through his mother, Isabella, daughter of Philip IV. As nephew rather than cousin Edward was nearer in blood to the last three kings. Although women had been excluded from the succession in 1317 nothing had been said about their right to transmit a claim to their male offspring. There is no proof that the French were at this time consciously following 'Salic Law'. The idea that Salic Law prevented women even transmitting claims was, it seems, largely invented by the French in the middle of the fourteenth century as retrospective justification for Valois tenure of the throne.[22] Thus in 1328 Edward had a claim worth advancing – even some French legal experts may have thought so – but we do not know whether his claim was considered at the assembly of 2 April.

Philip's swiftness in calling this assembly precluded attendance by Edward's representatives. There is no evidence that English envoys were appointed to go to Paris until 16 May. The written instructions then given to the bishops of Worcester and Coventry were rather imprecise, and the intentions of the English government in sending representatives at all remain equally vague for the historian.[23] Presumably it knew of the decision of 2 April that Philip should be king, yet the bishops were empowered 'to show, demand, request and require for us and in our name all the right actions and possessions of the kingdom of France which have come down to us and which belong to us ... as to a direct heir of the said kingdom', 'to make requests and demands for the right of the said kingdom to those who are occupied with the matter' and finally 'to accept *journe* (debate?) with all those who dispute that the kingdom should come to us'. Was this a claim to the throne or merely an opening diplomatic gambit, perhaps aimed at negotiating some territorial settlement? As the right to a share in the royal demesne had been admitted for other royal daughters, Isabella or her son might be deemed to have a similar claim to some French royal lands.

Apparently, Edward II had toyed with this idea on behalf of his wife in 1317.[24] Yet neither then nor in 1328 does this line of argument seem to have been put forward by the English, or exploited by them in order to bargain for sovereignty in Aquitaine. The bishops were unable to present their master's request because they were violently threatened by Philip's supporters. The claims of a foreign-born, untried youth with a notoriously unpopular mother, and ruler of territories so recently at war with Charles IV, were scarcely likely to be taken seriously. In addition the Valois family were no friends to the English: Philip had been involved in the making of the 1327 peace and his father, Charles (d. 1325), had led French attacks on the English in Gascony in 1294–5 and 1323–4.[25] By the time the bishops arrived in Paris the succession was no longer debatable; Philip VI was about to be crowned. The English had left it too late, perhaps because intelligence of events in France was poor, perhaps because there was little enthusiasm in England for the claim.

It is normally assumed that Isabella was behind the sending of the envoys on 16 May, but possibly Flemish townsmen, then in rebellion against their French-sponsored count, had encouraged it. Anglo-French war or, even better, an English king on the French throne, would have been to their benefit. When one of the rebels, William de Deken, was tried for treason in Paris later in 1328, he was charged that 'several times (since 13 April 1326) he had been in England to treat with the king that he be their lord in Flanders and also that he be king of France'.[26] He denied these charges, and there is considerable danger in taking them at face value, given the fraught state of Franco-Flemish and Franco-English relations in the late 1320s. By the time of the trial, Philip had defeated the Flemish rebels at Cassel (23 August 1328) and could thus afford to blacken both them and their supposed English friends. For the same reason French chroniclers saw fit to report rumours of Edward's intention to assist the Flemings during the ceremonies of the coronation.[27] It is true that the English were in contact with the Flemish rebels over the crucial period, but we do not know exactly what was discussed. Further contacts were also made with other Low Countries rulers, such

47

as Edward's father-in-law, Count William of Hainault. The latter's chronicler states that 'for a moment William of Hainault entertained some desire to support Edward as it would exalt his own daughter' but this may be patriotic retrospection, for the count soon showed himself loyal to his brother-in-law, Philip VI, attending the coronation on 29 May and sending troops to assist against the Flemish rebels.[28]

'Damp squib' seems to be an appropriate term for Edward's claim in 1328. If it was seriously entertained by Isabella and her party at this stage, why was it not followed up? Uncertainty of support in the Low Countries and the unreliability of the Flemish rebels may be factors. A significant consideration must have been the Scots, and here we return to the 'peace at all costs' policy. At the crucial moments of Philip's regency and accession the prime concern of the English government was negotiation of a peace with the Scots. This was finalised at Edinburgh on 17 March 1328 and ratified in Edward III's name at Northampton on 4 May.[29] This 'shameful peace', as it became known, recognised Robert Bruce as sovereign king of Scotland, thereby reversing English policy since the 1290s. Worse still, the treaty did not force the Scots to end their French alliance. Thus the most recent Franco-Scottish agreement made at Corbeil in 1326 still stood. This explicitly stated that any future Anglo-Scottish peace would be nullified if war broke out between France and England; the Scottish king would then be obliged to make war on the English irrespective of any truce or peace with them.[30] Isabella and Mortimer could not run the risk of a war with the French in 1328 for fear of a Scottish invasion; the Weardale campaign, which they had launched in response to the latest Scottish incursion in 1327, had proved an expensive fiasco.

Circumstances thus forced the French claim to be dropped. From May 1328 there were increased tensions between English and French seamen in the Channel, and by August rumours of an attack on the Channel Islands.[31] The situation in Gascony remained fragile; the native nobility expressed disquiet over the delayed restitution of, or compensation for, lands lost in the last war. In France there was no sign of support for Edward's claim to the French throne. Moreover, there was probably little enthusiasm for it in England, where the new regime was weak. Philip VI's government was by no means strong, but whereas the English government continued to weaken, his began to invigorate.[32] The failure on the part of the English to press Edward's claim was a notable factor in Philip's favour. He had exposed English weakness, and now had the opportunity to humiliate Edward further by demanding homage. He had to have Edward's homage for Aquitaine for this would confirm the latter's recognition of Philip as king and preclude any future claim to the French throne. It is no coincidence that Philip began to exert pressure for homage immediately after he had defeated the Flemish at Cassel on 23 August. Once again the English were in a weak position. The parliament of October 1328 seems to have urged that peace be kept with the French.[33] According to the *Grandes Chroniques*, Philip threatened that delay in performing homage might lead to the sequestration of Edward's revenues from the duchy – an interesting way of imposing pressure without recourse to full confiscation. This fear of loss of income, plus the possibility of a French invasion of the duchy, prompted the payment at least of simple homage for Aquitaine and Ponthieu by Edward at Amiens on 6 June 1329.[34] This he did according to the terms of the various treaties, but with the protestation that it did not diminish his rights to lands which had not been returned following the 1327 settlement. There was no specific mention of his right to the French throne, although in 1344 his ambassadors claimed that his homage at Amiens had not been intended to prejudge this issue.[35] To all intents and purposes and in the eyes of the rest of the world, Edward had formally recognised Philip as king of France by paying homage to him in 1329.

This did not solve problems in Gascony. French officials continued to act aggressively, partly because, as an English observer noted, Philip was not strong enough to stop them. He no doubt had little wish to because it was in his interests to keep Edward's position uncertain.[36] Over the next year, discussions failed to resolve outstanding questions of jurisdiction. In September 1330 Philip renewed pressure by demanding that Edward perform *liege* homage or lose his lands. At the end of the next month, Edward himself seized control of the English government. At first he continued his mother's policy, used too by Edward I and Edward II, of equivocation. Eventually he had to cave in: the French had attacked Saintes in December; Gascon defences were in a poor state; and there was reluctance in England to finance a war. On 30 March 1331 he confirmed his willingness to pay liege homage. Once again an English king had been outmanoeuvred, for it was clear that there was now little hope that the losses incurred in the war of 1324–7 would be restored. Edward did not in fact pay homage again but this was because Philip declared himself satisfied with Edward's confirmation that the homage of 1329 should have been liege. This admission could have ushered in an era of Anglo-French peace or at least of detente. The most hopeful sign of this was that the kings had a secret meeting later in 1331, where they agreed to try to sort out the issue of Aquitaine. Yet by 1337 they were at war once again. There are several reasons why this happened, but it is difficult to give much place to the continuing notion of a claim to the throne. Between May 1328 and the early months of 1337, when war was already unavoidable, there is no mention of the claim in English sources. Put simply, the claim was resurrected by the threat of war rather than being a cause of hostilities in its own right.

There are four major reasons why Philip and Edward went to war in 1337. One is that the Gascon situation did not improve. Appeals, threats and French infiltrations continued much as before, and the dispute over the Agenais reached an impasse in 1334. Even so, there was no particular reason to believe this would lead to immediate conflict, for Philip and Edward were still prepared to submit their differences to papal moderation and to consider a joint crusade. Events of the last fifty years or so had proved the Gascon situation to be well nigh insoluble, but it could perhaps have rumbled on for years as a kind of 'cold war'.

Other catalysts were required to provoke all-out war in 1337. The first was the reopening of the Anglo-Scottish war in 1333, the significance of which will be considered in greater detail in chapter 4. A few aspects of the Scottish situation need to be mentioned here, however. When he went to war with the Scots in

1332, Edward justified his breaking of the Treaty of North-ampton by claiming it was invalid as it had been made whilst he was a minor. The same argument was used in 1344 to explain to papal negotiators why he had not claimed the French throne before 1340. The excuse is also implicit in his Ghent declaration of 1340 where he claimed that Philip had intruded himself into the kingdom 'whilst we were yet of tender years'.[37] With hindsight it appears that his youth was a useful rather than a true argument, for Edward himself chose not to pursue the French claim from 1330 to 1337, and had invaded Scotland only when he saw Edward Balliol looked like defeating Robert Bruce's son, David II. Another important aspect of the Scottish wars – perhaps the most important – was that David received sanctuary and support in France. A proposed settlement over Gascony in 1334 was aborted when Philip insisted that the Scottish issue should be embraced within any Anglo-French peace.[38] This can be dismissed as mere warmongering on his part, but Philip may have felt bound both by honour and by treaty to help his Scottish allies. Edward was furious at Philip's interference in what he himself considered to be domestic affairs. He certainly mentioned this in his justification for war with France in 1337.[39] Moreover, his Scottish war went badly. Thus, when all the other issues in Anglo-French relations came to a head in 1336–7, Edward was touchy about Philip's support for the Scots, for this gave the French an excuse to launch raids on England. In this last respect the Hundred Years War differed from all previous conflicts with France in that from the start it involved French attacks on England, not just on Aquitaine.

The second catalyst was papal policy. Benedict XII desired peace in Europe partly to facilitate plans of a crusade. Whilst Philip seems to have been genuinely committed to the crusade, Edward was lukewarm, and never even symbolically took the cross.[40] On the other hand, each could use crusading plans to his particular advantage in Anglo-French negotiations. Edward thus argued that his participation in a joint crusade was dependent upon an agreement being reached over Gascony and on his being given a free hand in Scotland. For his part, Philip could portray Edward as being unreasonably obstructive in the crusading cause. As no settlement over Gascony or Scotland had been reached, and there were problems in Italy and Germany, Benedict postponed the crusade in March 1336, apparently to Philip's chagrin. In September the latter diverted his crusade fleet from Marseilles to the Channel ports, making it look very much as though an invasion of England was planned, presumably in aid of the Scots. It is hard to dispute Tyreman's conclusion that 'Benedict's cancellation itself pushed Western Europe nearer war'.[41] Moreover, it diminished the pope's potential role as peacemaker. The crusade cancelled, an Anglo-French war was rendered much more likely; both Edward and Philip stepped up their scramble for allies over the autumn and winter of 1336.

Into this scenario came the final *casus belli*, Robert of Artois. As an individual his role is much more difficult to assess than that of the 'issues' already considered, although recent commentators have urged that it should be taken seriously.[42] Robert was Philip's cousin and brother-in-law, and had enjoyed the king's favour at the outset of the reign. Relations were irrevocably soured when his aunt's inheritance to the county of Artois was preferred to his own, and when his recourse to forgery in pursuit of his inheritance was uncovered. Accused of his aunt's murder, he was dispossessed and condemned to death by Philip in 1332, but escaped to the Low Countries. Between 1334 and 1336 he came to England and was well received by Edward. One element in his significance is proven: Philip's confiscation of Aquitaine on 24 May 1337 was on the grounds that his ducal vassal, Edward, was harbouring Robert, despite a summons in December 1336 that he should surrender him to French justice. Another element is more difficult to prove, that Robert may have encouraged Edward to reconsider his claim to the French throne, perhaps by alerting him to his loss of honour in not pursuing his rights, and by persuading him of potential support in France.[43] There is no firm evidence of Robert's role, however. Whilst the honour argument might have cut some ice, Robert's suggestion that there would be support for Edward in France was surely less credible. The French nobility had scarcely sprung to Robert's defence and were even less likely to rally to Edward.

War was already inevitable. It had started in Gascony and the

Channel before the confiscation of the duchy in May 1337. Both sides had been firmly committed to conflict from the autumn of 1336, although Philip's actions identify him as the principal aggressor. The attempts at justification then began. For Philip it was wise to concentrate on Edward's vassalage in Aquitaine, for this was where the latter's vulnerability lay. The harbouring of Robert was deliberately manipulated to this end. The summons for his surrender in December 1336 was delivered to Edward through the seneschal of Gascony. Robert was in fact being sheltered in England but Philip could scarcely interfere with Edward's rule in his own kingdom. The subsequent confiscation of Edward's duchy and his county of Ponthieu was thus of dubious legality but served its purpose.[44]

Edward was also justifying his position. If the *Historia Roffensis* is to be believed, there was a meeting of the royal council in the Tower on 23 January 1337 to discuss 'the right which the king had to the crown of France'. This may be redatable to the Lent parliament of 1337, after which envoys were commissioned to go to 'Philip of Valois'. This is the first known use of this derogatory form in England, although it is interesting to note that the emperor, Lewis of Bavaria, had spoken in July 1336 of 'Philip who calls himself king of France'.[45] Yet despite such insults to Philip, Edward hesitated in actually claiming the French throne for himself at this stage. It is difficult to fathom what role thoughts of the claim played in his policies before January 1340. Even when Philip confiscated the duchy, Edward still accepted his kingship. The manifesto produced for circulation throughout England in late August 1337 stressed how the king of France had usurped Edward's rights in Gascony, had refused overtures of peace, and had assisted the Scots against Edward's interests. Significantly here the terminology spoke of Edward's rights in the duchy as king of England, not as duke, implying that he was already entitled to full sovereignty in Aquitaine. But it did not say that Edward was due to such sovereignty because of his right to the French throne; of this claim there was no mention.[46]

According to Froissart (who was writing with the advantage of thirty years or more hindsight), Edward's defiance to Philip, sanctioned by parliament in October and delivered to Paris in November 1337, claimed the throne. There is, however, no official record that Edward did more in 1337 than disavow his vassalage on much the same grounds as Edward I had done in 1298 – because of the non-fulfilment of the 1259 treaty and the allodial nature of Gascony.[47] A similar problem surrounds Le Baker's unique comment that, in negotiations with the cardinals during March 1338, Edward was prepared to surrender his claim to the throne in return for the peaceful possession of Aquitaine and his other fiefs, and for an end to French aid to the Scottish rebels.[48] According to diplomatic evidence, the idea of 'trading-in' the French claim in return for full sovereignty in Aquitaine only became English policy in the early 1350s.

Likewise, there is nothing to suggest that Edward saw a claim to the throne as a way around the problem of homage – what Chaplais calls the 'ideal solution', that being king of France would make Edward his own suzerain in Gascony.[49] In some ways the claims to full sovereignty and to the French crown were complementary, and perhaps even conflicting. Even if he were to claim the throne Edward could scarcely drop all the old notions developed since 1294 about the English king's right to full sovereignty by virtue of the allodial status of Gascony. If Gascony was an allod then Edward as putative king of France had no more authority in it than his Capetian predecessors! As we shall see, the Gascons and the English parliament expressed concern in 1340 that the assumption of the title 'king of France' might interfere with their own liberties. It is interesting to note, therefore, that when Edward did briefly assume the French royal title on 7 October 1337, he used his ducal title alongside it. The letters drawn up on this day – in the name of Edward as king of England and France, lord of Ireland and duke of Aquitaine, commissioning the duke of Brabant, the margrave of Juliers, the count of Hainault and the earl of Northampton as his lieutenants and vicars-general in France – are baffling.[50] Were they ever issued in France? Were they aimed at providing justification for the Low Countries' rulers to support Edward in his wars with Philip? Edward did not use the title again until January 1340. Other letters issued on 7 October 1337 did not include the

French title. Between 1337 and 1339 Edward sometimes referred to Philip as 'of Valois', and sometimes as king of France. On occasion two sets of letters were issued using these alternative appellations.[51] Even in his letter to the pope in July 1339, Edward explained why he had a claim to the French throne without explicitly putting it forward; he still stressed Philip's usurpation of his rights in Gascony and interference in Scottish affairs.[52]

It is difficult to avoid two significant conclusions, first that until 1340 Edward was reluctant to go very far in his claim to the throne, and secondly, that he was inconsistent and indecisive in his early war aims. Several explanations can be suggested: deference to papal peace initiatives; a lack of enthusiasm for the claim in England and Gascony; uncertainty over allies in the Low Countries; insecurity over the validity of the claim given that 1328 was now long past, combined, perhaps, with thoughts that it was not worth making because it could not be made effective in France. The role played by the emperor, Lewis of Bavaria, may also be significant in Edward's hesitation. A chronicle account says that at his meeting with Edward at Cologne on 5 September 1338, Lewis declared the king of France (i.e. Philip) forfeit. Yet Edward was not named king instead of Philip, being given instead the title of imperial vicar-general 'in Germany and France'.[53] It is not clear whether Lewis unequivocally recognised Edward as King of France. Lewis could only dissolve Philip's rule, and give Edward authority, in those small areas of northern France (around Cambrai) which lay within the Empire. The vicar-generalship had the principal advantage of enabling Edward to summon to arms Lewis's vassals in the Low Countries. These included the duke of Brabant, the margrave of Juliers, and the count of Hainault, but despite the letters of 7 October 1337 it is not entirely certain whether these princes definitely recognised Edward as French king at this stage. The first campaign against Philip, which eventually got under way in September 1339, was consciously limited to the Cambraisis. Edward issued orders in that area of northern France as vicar-general, not as king of France. A brief sortie into France was a failure, partly because the count of Hainault refused to

attack the ruler he recognised as legitimate king of France –
Philip.

Why did Edward abandon uncertainty and formally assume
the title at Ghent in January 1340? The most obvious explanation, perhaps, is that the alternative policies he had pursued
since 1337 had not met with success. Edward was in great
danger of losing the war, even the war for Gascony let alone any
bolder project. Admittedly the French had not made as much
headway in Gascony as might have been expected; in that
respect Edward's efforts on the northern frontier, which had
served to divide Philip's attention and military resources, had
saved the duchy from the fate which had befallen it in 1294. But
the duchy remained vulnerable, the Scots were still causing
problems and there had been increasingly serious French raids
on the south coast in 1338–9. The imperial vicariate had not
proved a great advantage. It had not given Edward victory in
the first campaign, nor had it prevented support for Philip in the
Low Countries.

More significantly, it had not persuaded either the Flemish
towns or their count, then in an uneasy state of reconciliation, to
come to an alliance with Edward. There was a real danger that
Philip would win over the Flemish by offering to return the
towns of Lille, Douai, Béthune, Cassel and Courtrai confiscated
by Philip IV in 1305. In his negotiations of November and
December 1339, Edward thus offered the count these towns in
return for his homage. In effect this was tantamount to claiming
the throne, for the towns lay within France and not within the
purview of his imperial vicariate, and it is clear that the only
homage the count was being asked to pay was to Edward as king
of France.[54] In early December the count fled to Paris in the face
of renewed urban revolt in Flanders, but Edward continued to
negotiate with the townsmen's 'guardian of the county', who was
already in receipt of an English pension. Agreement was reached
in early January when Edward bought the support of the
Flemish by various promises: to maintain the wool staple (the
exclusive market for English wool) in either Flanders or Brabant;
to allow duty-free import of Flemish cloth into England; to pay
large sums to Ghent, Bruges and Ypres; to offer protection if the

pope or Philip punished them for their revolt; to provide naval aid; and to return the lost towns and the county of Artois.[55]

Once the terms had been settled, Edward was received in splendour in Ghent where he assumed the arms and title of king of France on 26 January. Did he do this at the behest of the Flemish? Le Bel implies that he did, and a papal informant was convinced of it.[56] Indeed, the acceptance of Edward as king of France did offer the towns a useful means of justifying rebellion against their count. Yet there is evidence to suggest that both Edward and van Artevelde, leader in Ghent, hoped that the events of January 1340 would encourage the count to return and accept Edward as his French royal overlord. To this end, Edward had offered his daughter in marriage to the count's son, proposing that the title to the lost towns be vested in the latter. He also generously allowed the count's bastard brother to be released without ransom, and in the process gained the latter's homage to him as king of France. Most significantly, Edward did not appoint another count. None of this was enough to bring about the count's defection but even this could be used to Edward's advantage. The count's rejection of Edward's generous offers could only serve to strengthen Edward's right to the direct allegiance of the Flemish. Once 'king of France', he immediately declared that all ecclesiastical processes against them should be annulled – this undermined the threat of papal excommunication for their rebellion against the count. At the same time he granted the Flemish considerable independence from royal interference. He knew enough about appeals to agree that they should not be prosecuted in any court outside the county. Already Edward was being forced to limit his potential authority as French king.

Edward desperately needed a Flemish alliance if he was to make any further headway on Philip's northern frontier and to protect English maritime interests. As Le Bel states, Edward knew that the Flemish could help him more than the rest of the world.[57] But he could only meet Flemish demands by declaring himself king. He had little choice if he wished to continue the war against Philip. To win Flanders he had to claim France. Significantly, however, he chose to date his French reign from

25 January 1340, the day before his entry into Ghent, perhaps to avoid the accusation that he had been made king by the Flemish. But it is interesting to note that he considered this the beginning of his French reign and that he did not date it from the death of Charles IV in 1328. Significantly too he did not keep his title 'duke of Aquitaine' as he had done in October 1337. The assumption of the French royal title in 1340 seems to have been intended as a new beginning in Edward's wars. And in one very important sense it was. Even though many of the Flemish nobility immediately defected to Philip, Edward was now accepted for the first time as king in part of France. On 8 February, invitations were issued to the lost towns to accept his rule; the campaigns of the spring and summer of 1340 were devoted to their recovery, the first actions to be aimed at royal France. On the same day Edward issued a declaration justifying his actions and inviting the people of France to submit to him by Easter next, although Philip's strong northern fortifications make it unlikely that this was widely circulated within France, if at all.[58] Edward promised to do justice to all men and to revive the good laws of Louis IX, offering not to impose unjust exactions, such as changes in the coinage, but to rule with the advice of the magnates of France. These clauses all referred to existing political issues in France. Edward was now speaking for the first time as French king rather than as a rebellious ducal vassal. He was portraying the war as being no longer for Gascony but for the French throne. The events of January 1340 thus changed the nature of the war but, as we shall see, did not make it any easier to fight or to win, or to settle by diplomacy.

1340–1369

Let us assess Edward's position in 1340. With a Flemish alliance he was potentially stronger than he had ever been. On 24 June, the destruction of much of the Franco-Castilian fleet at Sluys gave him an unexpected advantage in the Channel and much lessened the threat to England. There were also some successes in Gascony. But the campaign which Edward himself conducted from July in northern France failed. By September 1340 shortage of resources led him to accept a truce (made at Esplechin) until June 1341.[59] It was probably his allies' lack of enthusiasm which forced him in September 1341 to abandon plans for a second campaign based on Flanders.[60] His German and Low Country allies started to defect when Edward failed to pay them for their earlier services. Soon after the truce was agreed, Emperor Lewis began negotiations with Philip and by April 1341 he had withdrawn the imperial vicariate from Edward. Even in England Edward faced problems. In March 1340 parliament sought assurances that his new French title would not lead to the subjection of England to France.[61] In June the Gascons had to be similarly reassured that the assumption of the crown would not affect their liberties.[62] In England new tax measures proved unpopular and impractical. Edward still owed thousands to Italian bankers and Low Countries' merchants. He thus found himself in a serious financial and political crisis on either side of the Channel.[63]

No support was forthcoming from the pope, who made clear his opinion that Edward's claim was unjust and impractical.[64] As for Philip VI, there is no doubt that he was incensed by Edward's assumption of the title. In the papally-sponsored negotiations at Avignon in 1344, Philip instructed his ambassadors to concentrate solely on the old issue of Gascony. After the failure of these talks, he created his own son duke of Guienne, thereby denying Edward's rights even to the duchy, let alone to the French crown. So outraged was he by Edward's presumption – all the more so after the defeat at Crécy in 1346 – that for the rest of his life Philip refused to entertain negotiations, although he was willing to come to truce.[65] Despite his lack of progress in Gascony, he was in a strong position in the early 1340s, regaining allies in the Low Countries and persuading the pope to excommunicate the Flemish. In 1341 he sponsored the return of the Scottish claimant, David II, thus stirring up further trouble for Edward in Scotland and encouraging the renewal of raids on northern England.

Assumption of the French title, therefore, did not strengthen Edward's position – rather the opposite, for it raised new problems and created an even greater impasse in Anglo-French relations. Yet we can also see by their reactions that the French, the English, the Gascons, the papacy and the rest of Europe took his claim much more seriously than they had before 1340. But did Edward? Did he really think he could become – did he wish to become – king of France? Le Bel's comments on the events of Ghent are of interest here; 'when he heard this report [of Flemish offers if he would take up the title] he needed much good advice, for it was a very significant and onerous thing to take the arms and name of what he had not yet conquered and what he did not know whether he could conquer ... but having thought long and hard, weighing the pros and cons, he took up the French [coat of] arms'. Le Bel clearly wished to stress that Edward had not acted either impetuously or without realisation of the likely repercussions of his action. This sentiment has been echoed by Le Patourel who considered that 'Edward was no fool. If he had really made the throne of France his war-aim, he must have felt that he had some chance of success.'[66] After all, he had already met with some success in Flanders, a key area for both claimants to control; he was not to know in 1340 that by 1345–6 political upheavals there would undermine his authority. There again, he could not have foreseen in 1340 the opportunities which would present themselves in Brittany through the succession dispute at the death of Duke John III on 30 April 1341. Once Philip had decided in favour of one of the claimants, Charles of Blois, Edward was bound to support the other, John de Montfort. According to Le Bel, Philip was alert to the danger which could ensue to his kingship if the duchy fell under Edward's control.[67] Edward was equally aware of the advantages which involvement in Brittany offered. It provided him with a valuable military base now that his position in the Low Countries was faltering. As soon as Edward offered military support to de Montfort he demanded in return the right to install his own troops and to draw upon ducal revenues to support them. Moreover it offered him another area – an area most emphatically within royal France – where his claim to the French throne might be recognised. Not surprisingly, therefore, Edward poured in troops and crossed to the duchy in person in 1342. From 1345 to 1362, with de Montfort's young heir in England, the duchy was ruled by Edward as king of France through an English captain-general whom he had appointed. The continuing state of civil war, however, meant that it was never totally or securely in his hands.

It can be argued that Edward's first campaigns of the Hundred Years War were waged in defence of the interests of others: the emperor and his Low Country allies in 1339, the Flemish in 1340 and de Montfort in the early 1340s. From 1345 to 1360, however, he acted on his own initiative, moving most emphatically on to the offensive and raising many more troops in England for his enterprises in France. As a result the war took on a rather different nature. This is one of the best known periods of the Hundred Years War, because it saw two great English successes in what was the fairly rare phenomenon of a major pitched battle – Edward's own victory at Crécy in August 1346 and that of his son at Poitiers ten years later. We must remember, however, that save in Brittany, military activity was restricted to only a few years – 1345–7, 1355–6 and 1359–60 – with periods of truce intervening. Even so the geographical spread of action was extensive, in a way that it had never been in the wars of 1294–7 and 1324–7. Edward sought to maintain several war theatres simultaneously. Brittany and Flanders continued to engage his attention. After Earl (later Duke) Henry of Lancaster had successfully secured and expanded English holdings in the south in 1345, Gascony too could be used as a useful launching pad for penetration into what was undeniably French royal territory. Thus campaigns were launched in 1346 and again in 1356 into Poitou, which had been given up in the Treaty of Paris of 1259 and never subsequently claimed. In 1355 the Black Prince led his troops from Bordeaux into the Toulousin, an area which had never been absorbed into the Angevin lands despite Henry II's efforts. In 1346 Edward III invaded Normandy, which had also been given up in 1259. He ruled Brittany as king of France and took homage from all its ducal claimants, even from Charles of Blois after his capture in 1347.[68] None of these areas had been claimed by an English king since 1259, and they had all been out of English hands for even longer.

Is it mere coincidence that all of the territories mentioned were once under the thrall of the Angevins? Was Edward consciously trying to revive the Angevin Empire rather than aiming to conquer France? He never expressed the first desire, although Ormrod has recently pointed to his interest in the deeds of Henry II during the early 1340s.[69] On certain occasions between 1356 and 1360, he seems to have used the title 'duke of Normandy' in addition to his French title.[70] In the draft treaties of 1354 and 1359, the lands to be accorded to him in full sovereignty read much like the old Angevin territories, and indeed the chronicler Henry Knighton claimed that in 1357 the papal negotiators offered him the lands of his ancestors.[71] It is possible, of course, that this aim was not in Edward's mind when he took up his French title in 1340 but gradually developed over the 1340s and 50s.

There are some dangers in assuming that Edward's aim was to restore the old Angevin Empire. The first is that the territories invaded were strategically those one would concentrate upon from bases in England, Gascony and Brittany, for ease of transport, access to the further regions of France and control of the Channel seaboard. Secondly, Edward's campaigns were not restricted to the old Angevin lands. Most certainly his ambitions stretched further than the restoration of Aquitaine to its 1259 boundaries. It is significant that he never went to the duchy in person. After all, he considered it his already as king of England, and there was still enough loyalty to him in Gascony to minimise the need to send large numbers of troops for its defence. Indeed the military service of the Gascons formed an important contribution to the expeditions which Lancaster and the Black Prince led out of the duchy. All Edward's major campaigns were fought in land ruled unequivocally by Philip. The English style of campaign – the *chevauchée* – can be seen as entirely appropriate for a claimant to the throne; it aimed at demonstrating Edward's might in as wide an area as possible, thereby undermining Philip's authority and challenging his right to rule. In the 1346 campaign Edward came as close to Paris as he could before being forced by French resistance to turn north. Following the victory at Crécy on 26 August 1346 he took Calais, to which he had no claim save as king of France. In 1350 he may have planned a campaign to pre-empt the succession of John II, but was prevented from landing by the Castilian fleet.[72] In 1359 he certainly had a crown in his baggage and was making for Reims; the route of this campaign took him well outside his ancestral lands. Even his use of the ducal title in Normandy may not have been aimed at emphasising ancestral connections. It is significant that it was taken up in 1356 rather than in the 1346 campaign. By 1356 there was virtual civil war in Normandy between the supporters of John II and his heir Charles, who had been granted the duchy in December 1355, and of Charles of Navarre. The latter had ambitions for a Norman principality as his price for allegiance to King John and had already been in negotiation with the English. Edward hoped to exploit this situation as he had in Brittany by encouraging defections to him rather than to either of the French princes. In their turn, some of the Normans, most notably Navarre's supporter, Geoffrey de Harcourt, sought to use Edward to their own ends against John II.[73] Edward's use of the Norman title in his dealings with the Normans was a further insult to the Valois, as the title had been held by the heir to the French throne since 1332.

The most judicious conclusion we can reach, perhaps, is that Edward was an opportunist. He would take whatever came his way, much as he had done before 1340 in his dealings with the Scots, the emperor and the Flemish. If military success and French noble defections had enabled him to depose Philip or John then he would surely have done so. As Le Bel pointed out, Edward did not know in 1340 whether he would be able to conquer France. It seems, however, that he did not hesitate to make war there. As his success mounted so the desire to make war became self-reinforcing. For Edward and for his people the waging of war against France became an end in itself. Peace negotiations in 1344, 1352–4 and 1358–9 failed because Edward refused to drop his claim to the throne. The fact that major campaigns followed all of these negotiations suggests that he hoped further military activity would bring him greater gain and glory.

Yet to conquer the whole of France was a formidable, and effectively impossible, task. Except in Brittany and at Calais,

Edward did not conquer territory. He and his captains led raids into French lands and sacked French towns but they did not leave behind an occupying army as Henry V was to do in the next century. Within a year of the Norman campaign of 1346, for instance, Prince John was back in virtually complete control of the duchy. The failure to install garrisons may well be explained simply by a lack of resources; it is clear that the defence of Calais was a major drain on English revenues throughout its tenure. But it may also suggest that Edward's plan was to harass the French into some kind of settlement, rather than to conquer territory. Here we must not forget the strength of French resistance to him, which was much greater and much more united than in the time of Henry V. It is all too easy to be seduced by the English successes at Crécy and Poitiers, but neither victory won Edward the war. Indeed they may have made him even less acceptable to the French people and encouraged a rallying behind their Valois ruler.[74] Likewise a successful *chevauchée* did not guarantee that the population would henceforth regard Edward as king. As *chevauchées* were largely aimed at the civilian population they could have rather the opposite effect on public opinion. Only a handful of Frenchmen ever formally accepted his kingship.[75] Deals were struck with some French nobles, but here the significant word is 'deal' for something had to be offered in return. The support of Charles of Navarre, who himself had a claim to the throne as the son of Jeanne, daughter of Louis X, could only be bought at the cost of a proposed division of France.

It remains difficult to assess how seriously Edward took his claim to the throne of France after 1340. He certainly invested considerable amounts of time, men and money in his campaigns but his actions suggest that he was not so much a man of principle as an opportunist and a realist. He was thus able to accept that he could not conquer the whole of France. But he could dismember it. This may have been his plan all along, although in the documentary sources this idea seems to have originated with papal negotiators and John II. At the peace negotiations at Guînes in April 1354, John II, more willing to negotiate than his father and worried at the prospect of an

Anglo-Navarrese alliance and further English successes, seemed prepared to offer Aquitaine, Poitou, Normandy, Anjou, Maine, Ponthieu and Calais in full sovereignty in return for a renunciation of Edward's claim to the throne.[76] The first and second Treaties of London (January 1358 and 24 March 1359) also envisaged a division of France. The second was similar to the Guînes proposal but added the homage of Brittany; the first offered only the southern lands but did not oblige Edward to renounce his royal claim.[77]

We must not forget that in the late 1350s Edward was faced with a grave dilemma. John II had been captured at the Black Prince's victory at Poitiers (19 September 1356). Although this strengthened Edward's negotiating position in some ways, it also served to complicate it. The capture of John laid open the prospect of a large ransom; 4 million *écus* was the asking level in the two London treaties. But to take a ransom implied acceptance of John's kingship. Edward followed this line in the main, for he knew from John's negotiations in London that the French king was prepared to make substantial territorial concessions. But he also clearly intended to pursue to the utmost the opportunity which John's capture provided. He thus still hoped to exploit French weakness to the limit, as the March 1359 terms show. Indeed he may have deliberately set these so high that the Dauphin Charles's government in Paris would reject them.[78] This refusal gave Edward the excuse to invade again in October 1359. He now made for Reims – ever the opportunist. He might after all succeed in being crowned, but even if he did not, his campaign would serve to put further pressure on the French to accept his terms for a territorial settlement which was effectively a dismemberment of Valois France.

To this end he raised an army of 12,000 in England, second only in size to the 32,000 deployed at the siege of Calais, and not matched again in English campaigns in France until 1475. But his plan misfired. The campaign was too late in two senses. It was waged over a particularly harsh winter, and its failure weakened rather than strengthened his position. It came three years after John's capture, during which time the French had slowly solved the problems of social and governmental dislocation which this had caused. Had Edward not been seduced by the prospect of a large ransom, had he not been caught by notions of chivalry towards John, had he made for Reims in 1356–8, he might have been crowned king. It is unlikely, however, that such a coronation would have ended the need for English military involvement in France.

In 1360 Edward gave up his French title. If the crown had been his principal objective in 1359 then he had failed. What he did succeed in doing was to dismember France. Here, however, the relative failure of his recent campaign forced him to reduce the demands he had put forward in March 1359 and to return essentially to the terms of the draft first Treaty of London of January 1358. The opportunist had not succeeded; the realist saw that he could put no further pressure on the French. He could scarcely raise another army on the scale of that of 1359. By the Treaty of Calais (24 October 1360, based on terms agreed at Brétigny on 8 May), Aquitaine, Poitou, Ponthieu, Guînes, Calais and its march were to be his in full sovereignty, and John was to be ransomed for 3 million *écus*.[79] In return Edward was to renounce his claim to the French throne and to Normandy, Anjou and Maine. Save for the reduction of the ransom, these were the terms of the first Treaty of London. But there was a further problem. At the time of the signing of the Treaty of Brétigny/Calais, not all of the promised territories were in Edward's hands. In order to guarantee that the French would hand them over, Edward seems to have had separated from the main body of the Treaty of Calais the clauses concerning renunciations – his own renunciation of the French throne, and French renunciation of sovereignty over Edward's extended landholding in France. Thus his giving up of the French title became dependent on his receipt of the territories in full sovereignty. The separate document (termed the *c'est assavoir* from its opening words) envisaged the transfer of the lands by 24 June 1361 or at least by 1 November following, with the renunciations being made orally, and then ratified in writing by 15 August or 30 November.[80] In the interim the French king was to refrain from exercising sovereignty in the territories and Edward was to drop his French title.

Much has been made of the significance of the separation of

the *c'est assavoir* clause. Because the mutual renunciations were never performed, it was possible for Charles V to claim in December 1368 that he still exercised sovereignty over Aquitaine and could thus hear appeals. This led in 1369 to the confiscation of the duchy, to Edward's resumption of the French title, and to a new war. It seems unlikely, however, that Edward deliberately separated the clause in 1360 to give him a loophole to revive his claim to the throne.[81] As suggested above, he did it to ensure that all the territories promised would come into his hands. By the time the clause was separated from the main body of the treaty Edward had already committed himself to surrendering his title. By agreeing to ransom John and by coming to treaty with him he had recognised his kingship. From 24 October 1360 Edward stopped using the French title even though the transfers of land had not been completed. Admittedly Edward never formally renounced his French title, but John's kingship was never subsequently denied by Edward even after war recommenced in 1369, nor was there any English doubt that Charles was king of France from his accession in 1365 to the resumption of the title by Edward on 3 June 1369. Moreover, Edward did surrender to the French the few fortifications he held in Normandy, Anjou and Maine over the course of 1360–1. We can suggest, therefore, that Edward intended the Brétigny/Calais settlement to be effective and that John II did too, for he never denied his ransom obligations. Both sides therefore saw the settlement as tenable and as a full, negotiated treaty, the first since 1327. It was intended to mark the end both of Edward's claim to the throne and of French sovereignty in his continental possessions.

Edward's principal concern from 1360 was the exercise of full sovereignty over his lands in France. Under the wartime conditions which had prevailed since 1337 he had enjoyed this *de facto*, setting up arrangements whereby Gascon appeals could be heard by the English parliament.[82] It continued to be his main concern into the early 1360s when he tried to put pressure on John, through the members of the French royal family who had been provided as hostages for the payment of the ransom, to perform his side of the renunciations.[83] Edward may have regarded sovereignty as his without the renunciations, for he had

67

mention of it dropped also from the main body of the treaty – another form of insurance perhaps.

In Edward's eyes the treaty of 1360 was a victory. It is later historians who have seen it as a climb-down. Through a combination of a useful if unfulfillable claim to the French throne and considerable military success over twenty years, Edward had forced the French to accept his terms, thus winning for himself direct rule over a sizeable part of France. He might have surrendered the title of king of France but in the territories confirmed to him he remained a *king*, albeit king of England. The Treaty of Brétigny/Calais did not oblige him to rule his French lands in any other way. From 1360 the administration of Calais, Guînes and Ponthieu was thus carried out in his English royal title. There is some evidence that he may have envisaged the elevation of Aquitaine into a separate kingdom.[84] Yet he never did so, entitling himself rather as 'Lord of Aquitaine'. This may have been out of respect for Gascon liberties, which would have made the use of either 'King of Aquitaine' or 'King of England' unacceptable. The creation of an Aquitanian kingdom would surely have been unacceptable to the French and to the papacy, and would have been unconventional behaviour in medieval terms. One could not create new kingdoms at will. As the example of Ireland had already shown, there was no practical difference between the rule of a king and of a 'lord'. His (effectively royal) sovereignty in his French lands was given full expression by the granting of Aquitaine as a principality to the Black Prince in July 1362, in return for homage to his father and the annual payment of an ounce of gold as acknowledgement of the king's sovereignty. It is also confirmed by the prince's surrender of this grant to his father in April 1372, whereupon Edward resumed direct control of Aquitaine.[85] Over the ten years of his principality, the prince never had supreme authority in Aquitaine since his father retained the right to hear appeals. Subsequent events can be taken as indication that the problems of jurisdiction which had so dogged the king/duke before 1337 persisted under the new relationship of king/lord and prince. Edward's belief in his quasi-royal sovereignty in the lands confirmed to him in 1360 is also shown by his proposals in 1364 to settle the northern possessions of Calais and Ponthieu on his fourth son in return for homage to him as king of England.

This belief persisted in the minds of English kings well into the fifteenth century. Even though the French title was resumed and most of the Brétigny lands lost after 1369, Edward and his successors continued to consider the Brétigny settlement as applicable. Until 1420 the call of the English was for fulfilment of Brétigny, just as it had been, in the thirteenth and early fourteenth centuries, for the fulfilment of the Treaty of Paris of 1259. English kings might have been prepared to negotiate some changes, even perhaps to consider some non-degrading form of homage to the French king, or alienation to a collateral branch of the English royal family, but the basic stance on sovereignty never faltered.

Edward had achieved more than any of his predecessors could have envisaged. The land under his sovereign control was of greater extent than any English king had enjoyed since 1204. The wars and effective dismemberment of French royal territory gave him and his people an unprecedented military reputation in Europe. But they had also sharpened national stances and identity, the culmination of a process largely originating under Edward I. This is clearly revealed in the parliament of 1363 where the Commons thanked Edward for delivering them from 'servitude to other lands [i.e. France] and from the charges sustained by them in times past'.[86] Edward's star was in the ascendant at home and abroad. Over the 1360s he sought to maintain this position, and to damage French interests further, by throwing his weight around in Europe. His own intervention in Flemish affairs was matched by his son's involvement in Spain. In both areas, however, they failed in their objectives. Charles V (1365–80), less willing to adhere to Brétigny than his father, was able to outwit them and to restore French fortunes. By 1369, therefore, the English star was on the wane.

Had Edward achieved his aim in Flanders, English dominance of France would have been further enhanced.[87] His plan was to marry his fourth son, Edmund, to Margaret, only child of Louis de Mâle, count of Flanders. She stood to inherit Flanders, Nevers and Rethel from her father, the counties of

Burgundy and Artois from her paternal grandmother, and the duchies of Limburg and Brabant from her aunt. Edmund intended to settle Calais, Guînes and Ponthieu on Edmund and to pursue the claims of his queen, Philippa, to the counties of Hainault, Holland and Zeeland. Had the marriage and land settlement gone ahead, as the count's agreement to the treaty of Dover on 19 October 1364 suggested it would, Edward's influence would have held sway in a vast block of territory on the northern and western frontiers of France. John II had already tried to extend French interests in adjoining territories by having his youngest son, Philip, invested with the county of Burgundy in January 1362, and the duchy of Burgundy (the lands held within France by Margaret's first husband) in September 1363. Once the Dover terms were known, Charles V put pressure on Pope Urban V to refuse a dispensation for the marriage of Edmund and Margaret, and bribed Louis de Mâle with an offer to return the towns which the Flemish had lost to the French in 1305. The pope concurred and in 1367 permitted Margaret's marriage to Philip instead. In the following year Louis allowed this wedding to take place.

These French actions led to a deterioration in relations with England. As in the 1330s both sides sought allies in the Low Countries and Germany, but this time the French proved more successful, especially in their dealings with the emperor, Charles IV. Furthermore, Charles V had also defeated Charles of Navarre at Cocherel on 16 May 1364, forcing the latter to surrender his lands in the following year. Edward III had restored the duchy of Brittany to Duke John IV in 1362. In December 1365 the duke finally paid homage to the French king, thus loosening his ties with England. Although Louis de Mâle remained unreliable even after his daughter had married Philip of Burgundy, Charles could from 1368 look forward to the future succession of his son to the county of Flanders.

In Spain as in Flanders, things began well for Edward but ended disastrously.[88] In 1362 he secured an alliance with Pedro I of Castile which gave him use of the great Castilian fleet as a deterrent against potential French moves. Unfortunately Pedro was so paranoid that he tried to murder any rivals. His half-brother, Henry of Trastamara, took refuge in southern France where his cause was taken up by the duke of Anjou and by Bertrand du Guesclin. Their companies invaded Castile, deposed Pedro and installed Trastamara on the throne in 1365. Whether this was at French royal command is not clear: certainly the English suspected Charles V of connivance but it has never been categorically proven. Pedro fled to Aquitaine and sought English aid. Edward allowed the dispatch of 1000 men to assist the Black Prince's attempts to restore Pedro. The decision to intervene in Spain probably lay not so much with Edward as with the prince, who hoped to extend his own authority by accepting Pedro's promises of money and lands in Spain. As is well known from Froissart, the prince, with Aragonese assistance, defeated Trastamara at Nájera on 3 April 1367 and reinstated Pedro.

This victory proved costly. Pedro never recompensed his supporters, so that the cost of the campaign had to be met from taxation in Aquitaine. The Estates acquiesced in January 1368 to demands for a five-year levy, but this came on top of heavy taxation earlier in the 1360s. The prince's regime was declining in popularity as the drawbacks of the Brétigny settlement for the Gascons were revealed. Like the Scottish, the Gascons had benefited from earlier Anglo-French disputes. Before 1360 fears of French penetration had ensured a conciliatory attitude on the part of the English, particularly as the Gascons had played a major role in their own defence. Likewise, French desire to undermine English authority had prevented a heavy-handed approach from Paris. This relative independence had been destroyed by the Treaty of Brétigny and by the creation of a principality. For the first time since 1289 the Gascons had a resident lord with an expensive court and a desire to place in office those he had brought from England.[89] By 1368 it seems there were strains in the relationship between the people and their prince, who was himself in increasingly poor health.

There was, however, no open rebellion. Resistance to the prince's rule came from two lords, the count of Armagnac and the sire d'Albret, whose ancestors had always proved troublesome because they held some lands of the French king as well as others of the king/duke. They objected to the levying of the hearth tax on their lands in Aquitaine and sent an appeal against the prince to his father in England. Apparently on their own initiative – no French royal connivance has been proved – and without waiting for Edward's reply, they approached Charles V. Their behaviour echoed that of other Gascon lords in the past who had sought to further their own interests by exploiting the fragility of Anglo-French relations. Charles – no less an opportunist than Edward III – received them warmly: d'Albret was soon married to the French king's sister. The idea that they should make a formal appeal to Charles, along the lines of those common before 1337, rather than merely seek his direct military or diplomatic assistance, may well have come from the king or his advisers. Charles took legal advice about the possibility of his hearing such an appeal. He was told that since the renunciations of *c'est assavoir* had never been exchanged, sovereignty and *ressort* over Gascony had reverted to the French crown. On 30 June 1368 the count of Armagnac made his formal appeal against the Black Prince before the Paris *parlement*. Charles V offered the Gascon lords aid against any reprisals the prince might take but this offer remained secret. It was not until 3 December 1368 that Charles issued a proclamation that he was by law able to receive appeals. Moves were already being made to bribe further appellants. The Black Prince was issued with a summons to the Paris *parlement* in mid-January 1369. By the following May nearly 900 appeals had been engineered. The prince's failure to answer the summons (to which he is said to have reacted violently) led to his branding as a contumacious vassal on 2 May, although there was no formal confiscation until November. It is significant that the Black Prince – not the sovereign lord of Aquitaine – had been chosen as target in preference to Edward III. Charles had circumvented the Brétigny/Calais settlement.

Charles had clearly decided on war by the time of his declaration of 3 December 1368. In the previous month he sponsored the successful return to Castile of Henry of Trastamara. On 20 November the latter had agreed to an alliance whereby he promised naval aid to Charles if war broke out soon.[90] This treaty explicitly mentioned the possibility of the capture of anyone of English royal blood, and stated that any territory taken by Trastamara's men in the kingdom of England or in the duchy of Aquitaine should be given to the French king. Edward III sensed the danger but seems to have urged conciliation, suggesting that Charles should act as arbitrator between the Black Prince and his Gascon vassals, and that the mutual renunciations of the Brétigny/Calais settlement should now be performed. This was tantamount to admitting some degree of French right in the matter and shows Edward's fear of the outbreak of war. Edward certainly needed to play for time. Unlike Charles V, he was scarcely prepared for war. The English had seen no necessity to place large numbers of troops in the areas transferred to them in 1360 – a significant reflection of their belief that the Brétigny/Calais settlement would be permanent and undisputed. By early 1369 troops led by Charles's brother, Louis, duke of Anjou, had overrun the Rouergue; clergy there and in Quercy had begun to preach against the English, and a considerable number of castle-holding nobles had been won over to the French cause.

Before the declaration of contumacy on 2 May, the French had invaded Ponthieu. This was a direct insult to Edward himself and was thus cited as justification for the king's resumption of the French royal title in parliament on 3 June.[91] Charles was not called king of France on this occasion, although his father's kingship was admitted. Charles was charged with usurping the sovereignty of the king of England as granted in 1360 by a treaty to which he himself had pledged his oath. Much was made of the fact that Charles had already resorted to military attack, and that he was gathering ships to invade England, it was claimed, to overthrow Edward. With the unanimous consent of those assembled at the parliament, Edward resumed the title of king of France. Five days later, presumably in full knowledge of this, Charles announced his intention of making war against the Black Prince and his supporters, although Edward III was not named specifically. The English and French were once more at war.

1369–1399

Until the 1970s, British historians had shown little interest in this stage of the Hundred Years War, perhaps because the English did badly and there were no major battles. The work of Sherborne and Palmer has done much to redress this neglect. As Palmer points out, conflict from 1369 to 1399 was considerably more intensive than between 1337 and 1360.[92] In the earlier period there was the equivalent of fifteen years of truce, in the later only four, until hostilities finally ceased in 1389. The later period also saw longer campaigns, a wider geographical spread of fighting and considerably more action at sea. Threats to England also increased, and the wars had a greater impact on domestic politics. There can be no doubt that the English continued to take the war seriously: they were certainly still prepared to invest much money and manpower in it. Their military efforts after 1369 should not be written off as a pale reflection of former or later glories. Whilst much territory was lost, the French were never able to take it all, or to force the English into a disadvantageous settlement.

Edward was not prepared for war in 1369. He felt himself isolated and vulnerable, being without the set of alliances he had negotiated before contemplating hostilities in 1338. His treaty of 11 January 1369 with Aragon was no counterbalance to France's alliance with Castile of November 1368, which had already led to seaborne raids on southern England.[93] Moreover, he had justifiable worries about the loyalty of the Gascon nobility. He thus made considerable efforts to win their support, in June 1369 offering them the right to retain any conquests they might make from the French. In December he circulated in the duchy a manifesto condemning Charles V's actions against the Brétigny settlement.[94] Significantly, this was sent out in Edward's name. Likewise, in the previous month, the king had cancelled his son's much hated hearth tax. The Black Prince's rule of the duchy had not been a success, partly because of problems raised by non-royal tenure (which were to surface again in the 1390s), and partly because of his style of government. He continued to prove that he could not cope with failure. In 1370 he incurred opprobrium by sacking Limoges as punishment for its bishop's negotiations with the French – a gross misjudgement considering that the French had already met with considerable success in his principality. His health worsened, forcing him to return to England in 1371. In the following year he surrendered the principality, or what was left of it, to his father, who now set up a court of final appeal in Aquitaine to block the loophole exploited by the French in 1368–9. Until 1390 it remained in royal hands. There is as yet no full published study of this period of English rule in Gascony but what is known suggests that local politics continued to exercise an important influence on English policies, although it was partly due to the efforts of loyal Gascon subjects that the English were not driven out of the duchy altogether.

Put simply, the war from 1369 was over the Brétigny settlement rather than the French crown. Charles V was determined to overthrow the treaty because it diminished his royal authority. His initial campaigns thus concentrated on the conquest of English-held territory. Rouergue had already been overrun. By the end of 1369, Quercy, most of the Agenais, Périgord and Ponthieu had fallen. In 1370 the rest of the Agenais, the Limousin and Buzac were lost, and by the end of 1372 La Rochelle, Poitou, Saintonge and Bigorre had succumbed. La Réole surrendered in 1374 and even the Dordogne was penetrated in 1377. At that point, all of the gains in Aquitaine made by the English in 1360 had gone; they held only the coastal strip and its hinterland between Bordeaux and Bayonne, with a northern extension into the Médoc. The French made no further major gains after 1377, but neither did the English recover much territory. Thus, at the truce of 1396 and into the fifteenth century, English-held lands were virtually the same as those held by Edward III before war began in 1337. Calais was the only real exception, being retained in English hands despite threats to it in 1371–2 and in 1377. As in earlier periods, French gains were partly retained by the crown and partly distributed within the royal family: Poitou and Bigorre were given to Charles V's brother, the duke of Berry, and Périgord and Angoulême were subsequently granted to the duke of Orléans, Charles VI's brother. These grants symbolised the recovery of French sovereignty over the territories lost in 1360.

English war aims are more difficult to fathom. Let us examine these chronologically, commenting also on why the English met with less success than before. Edward appears to have remained committed to the terms of 1360; their fulfilment was still his demand in the negotiations of 1375–7. His resumption of the royal title in 1369 merely symbolised how the French had reneged upon the Brétigny settlement. Weak as he had been in 1340 with regard to his claim to the French throne, he was in an even weaker position in 1369. Only nine years earlier he had voluntarily surrendered the title on his own terms. Its readoption could now be interpreted as depending upon French non-fulfilment of Brétigny rather than on hereditary right. In 1369 the French king's hearing of Gascon appeals was a much more powerful and practical weapon than Edward's resumption of the title. Edward's credibility as a claimant to the throne or to sovereign territories was further undermined by the swift loss of lands.

Despite the losses, Edward continued to pursue an aggressive strategy. He was reluctant to fight a primarily defensive war: indeed, neither in Scotland nor in France did he ever successfully do so. Between 1369 and 1374 ambitious *chevauchées* were launched into northern France more frequently than ever, penetrating right into the heartlands of the French monarchy. The first, led by his third son, John of Gaunt, duke of Lancaster, traversed Artois, Picardy and Normandy. In 1370 Sir Robert Knollys raided around Paris into Brittany and Poitou. Three years later Gaunt led one of the longest *chevauchees* ever from Calais to Bordeaux, encircling Paris to the east through Champagne. Edward may have hoped that these actions would force Charles V to withdraw his armies from the attack on English lands and to come to battle. They were also intended as punishments for the latter's dishonourable actions. Edward's stance remained, in appearance at least, that of a challenger to the throne, although this does not prove that the crown was his principal objective. His aim was to crush the French into submission and negotiation, much as he had done in the 1350s.

Moreover, the *chevauchée* had served him well in his earlier wars.

But this time the effect on both sides was grinding rather than decisive. If the English were intent upon bringing the French to battle – an opinion widely held by historians but one which is in need of further detailed research – then they failed to do so. The French most certainly sought to avoid pitched battle: this laid the country open to damage and demoralisation and prevented French victory. But it did enable them to avoid defeat, which the events of the first wars had shown to be even more damaging and demoralising. The English were forced to spend year after year launching costly expeditions. Nine major expeditions left England between 1337 and 1360. Between 1369 and 1389, however, fourteen were despatched, often for longer periods of service than in the earlier phase of the war. These armies were also relatively more costly for they contained a greater proportion of men at arms than had earlier been the case.[95] The English too were ground down, particularly financially, by frequent expeditions which brought diminishing returns. Gascony remained vulnerable: more reinforcements had to be sent for its defence than in earlier periods, and there was an increasing need to launch naval expeditions and to protect merchant shipping.[96]

After 1369 there were two further weaknesses in the English position which had not been present in the earlier wars. The first was the problem of leadership. Edward never appeared in France again after 1360. In 1372 it was initially intended that he should lead an expedition to northern France but the threat posed by the Castilian fleet persuaded him instead to go to sea with over 6000 men, the largest army assembled between 1359 and 1415. In the event, bad weather prevented this force from ever setting sail. The Black Prince was too ill to fight, and Edward's own health deteriorated. As his son predeceased him, he was succeeded by his ten-year-old grandson, Richard II, who by virtue of his youth or of the policies of his advisers, never led a campaign to France, athough he did go to Ireland and Scotland. Whilst the war continued to be fought, at least in theory, for the crown of France, it was counter-productive for kings not to be personally involved. The claim to the throne had even less validity if they did not appear in France in person. In retrospect it can be seen that only those endeavours in France where a king was personally active were successful. In England, enthusiasm for the war, measured by the willingness to provide men and money, mounted when the kings themselves led expeditions. Royal-led armies were always considerably larger than those despatched under other captains. As we shall see, the attitude of the king was the crucial element in peace negotiations. By 1369 many of the former commanders had died or were too old. There were still men of the calibre to lead expeditions, but their activities were undermined by the lack of a single guiding royal hand. In the 1380s different groups pushed different war aims, thus dissipating the effects of military effort.

The second weakness derived from the issues of Scotland, Brittany and Spain. Edward had swiftly agreed to a 14-year truce with the Scots in June 1369, but the latter soon drifted back into the French camp, thus constituting a potential and sometimes an actual threat to English interests.[97] Edward soon found himself embroiled in Brittany again.[98] When the war opened, Duke John IV was an ally of the French but defected to the English at the end of 1372. This could have been a great advantage but it was not immediately exploited so that the French were able to overrun most of the duchy. Many English expeditions were sent to Brittany and the duke also led campaigns elsewhere. Much money was poured into bolstering the duke's control but as in the 1340s and 50s the duchy was never totally secured. In addition, internal Breton politics complicated the main Anglo-French war. In April 1381 Duke John made his peace with Charles VI. Although he specifically swore to oppose Richard II in his French pretensions, he remained largely neutral thenceforward. It is interesting to note that in 1380 Richard II conceded that if he ever became king of France the duke would not owe him homage. The ability to trade his adherence allowed more freedom to the duke than before. This form of Breton separatism remained a significant factor in Anglo-French relations well into the next century.

The Franco-Castilian alliance was particularly significant in naval terms because the Castilians had one of the largest and best-equipped fleets in Europe. This made the English coasts and merchant shipping more vulnerable than in any previous period, a fact which had considerable repercussions on public opinion. The Castilian fleet was responsible for scuppering the force sent to relieve La Rochelle in 1372 so that this key port, and with it the whole of Poitou, fell to the French, although Trasta-mara failed in his attempt to take Bayonne in 1374. In 1371, John of Gaunt married the daughter of Pedro I and thus had a claim to the Castilian throne, but Edward diverted Gaunt's first proposed attack of 1372 to further royal plans elsewhere.[99] Simi-larly, an expedition to Flanders was given priority in 1383 so that it was not until 1386 that Gaunt invaded Castile. The Spanish issue, like the Breton, complicated matters, particularly in the diplomatic sphere, because of French commitment to the Castilians and English commitments to the Aragonese and Portuguese.

Despite initiating some military and naval reforms and attempting to unite his country in the war effort, Charles V could not afford to take English invasions lightly. We know with hindsight that the English war effort failed but this was not so predictable at the time. It is significant that Charles felt it necessary to commission a fuller definition of Salic Law to justify the Valois inheritance, although perhaps more interesting for the current debate that no English counter-works are known. The English claim to the throne was of limited bargaining value once territory had been lost and repeated *chevauchées* had failed to bring the French to their knees. The weak position of the English is revealed by the negotiations at Bruges between 1375 and 1377 during a two-year truce. None of the proposals put forward by the papal negotiators offered as much as Brétigny. In fact they were similar to those advanced in 1344 before Edward had shown his strength: English abandonment of continental lands in return for compensation elsewhere; the severing of the direct link between the English crown and Gascony by its granting to one of Edward's younger sons who would hold it of the French king; the division of Gascony into parts which could be held in different ways to suit all parties.[100] Continuing commitment to Brétigny led the English to refuse to consider any diminution of territory or sovereignty. Recent military success and the hope of more to come made the French reluctant to give up their conquest or their feudal claims. The idea of a long truce foundered because of the lack of resolution of other conflicts in Brittany and Spain in which the English and French were embroiled.

The truce came to an end in June 1377, and Edward died on the twenty-first of the same month. The French sought to take advantage of this by stepping up raids on the south coast of England, invading the Dordogne and encouraging Gascon defections.[101] But the English managed to hold steady. Interest in France did not diminish and the nobility showed adequate enthusiasm for the war. The French remained the duplicitous enemy, a situation exacerbated by their support of a different pope in the papal schism which began in 1378. There was no thought that Richard II should not bear the French royal title, or not inherit the rights bestowed by Brétigny.[102] *Chevauchées* were not abandoned, but from 1378 more attention was given to the holding of well-defended ports on the western seaboard of France. This strategy was portrayed to parliament as being vital to the protection of England and the seas, on the grounds that war fought overseas had already proved to be the surest form of defence.[103] Calais was already held and provided the launching pad for several expeditions. Brest had been held by English troops from 1372, but in 1378 it was formally leased from the duke of Brittany and remained in English hands until 1397. Cherbourg was similarly handed over in the same year by the king of Navarre and held until 1393. Over the next four years, attempts were made to take Harfleur, St Mâlo, Nantes and La Rochelle but none met with success. Moreover, the costs to the English Exchequer of maintaining permanent garrisons in Calais, Cherbourg and Brest proved so high that the policy became less popular with parliament, given that the latter had probably accepted it in 1378 in the hope that it would prove cheaper than *chevauchées*.[104] Unremitting war taxation helped to cause the Peasants' Revolt of 1381. As Palmer points out, however, the third poll tax which sparked the revolt had some logic; it would have enabled the English to take advantage of Charles V's death (September 1380), which came shortly after a damaging English *chevauchée* from Calais through Champagne and Anjou to southern Brittany.[105]

Financial difficulties increasingly affected English military plans after 1381. These may have persuaded Richard's advisers of the need to take advantage of other quarrels in Flanders and Spain, where the English would not bear the whole burden of war. The towns of Flanders had once more risen against their count in 1379. There were hopes on both sides, for much the same reasons as in 1340, that Richard would be accepted there as French king.[106] But there was by no means the same support for an English claimant as in 1340 or the same advantages to be gained. The initial reluctance of parliament in 1382 to vote supply meant that the townsmen were defeated at Roosbecke on 27 November before a desultory English force arrived. This had been financed in preference to Gaunt's Castilian campaign, so both opportunities had been lost. In 1383 a church-funded 'crusade' to Flanders against the count's support for the French-sponsored pope in the schism foundered when the troops had to be evacuated Dunkirk-style. Although some aid was sent to Ghent when it rebelled against its new duke, Philip of Burgundy, in 1384–5, it was not enough to prevent his victory and the subsequent French domination of Flanders.

There was a brief truce in 1383–4. A three-year truce in June 1389 came to mark the end of hostilities. What happened in between is extremely complicated as political problems in England became inextricably linked with policies abroad. Richard's authority was placed in commission in November 1386, passing into the hands of a group of magnates (the Appellants) in late 1387. Not until May 1389 did the king regain control of his government. Confusion over policy was exacerbated by Gaunt's ambitions in Castile. In 1385–6 the English position was perhaps at its lowest ebb. Initiatives in Flanders had failed. There were real threats of coordinated French and Scottish invasions. Sherborne suggests that this reveals a change in French policy, moving away from occasional raids to outright invasion.[107] It was certainly encouraged by the fact that Flanders could now be used as a base to launch an attack. Against the Scots the largest military initiative since 1335 was deemed necessary, for which recourse had to be made to the feudal levy, last used in 1327, probably because funds were too low to finance a large contract army.[108] Initially, the English looked able to redeem their position. The 1385 expedition succeeded in containing the Scots; the French called off their invasion, and Portuguese allies scored a victory against Trastamara at Alijubarrota on 14 August 1386. Gaunt's subsequent campaign in Castile, however, was a failure and the English government found itself in a serious financial crisis. Parliamentary hostility to voting further taxation is witnessed by the impeachment in November 1386 of the chancellor, Michael de la Pole, after his request for four times the standard tax levy.[109] These tax demands may reveal a plan to invade France in the hope that this would prevent French attacks on England.[110] Yet de la Pole was also involved in attempted peace negotiations in 1386. There were growing indications of divergence of opinion over the war, with some signs that the king himself was moving in favour of a negotiated settlement.[111]

Whether the placing of Richard's authority in commission was a reaction to this is unclear. It cannot be doubted, however, that the Appellants began their period of control by pursuing an aggressive line. In 1388 they developed plans to launch campaigns in Flanders with the aid of the duke of Guelders, into Brittany with the aid of Navarre and possibly with the connivance of the duke himself, and into Gascony under Gaunt. One of the Appellants, the earl of Arundel, set sail in June 1388 with 3500 men to raid the Norman and Breton ports, but the duke of Brittany did not come to his aid as hoped; a subsequent attack on La Rochelle also failed. In July Gaunt abandoned his claim to the Castilian throne in return for a pension and the marriage of his daughter to Trastamara's son, thus making negotiations with the French easier.[112] In August the Scots inflicted another blow to English pride at Otterburn. Thenceforward, the Appellants moved towards diplomacy, reversing their previous stance. When Richard II recovered his authority on 16 May 1389, he accepted the three-year truce which the Appellants had begun to negotiate. This marked the longest cessation of hostilities since 1369.[113] Thenceforward Richard was committed to a peace policy. Later historians have seen him as being prepared to give up his French title and even to pay some sort of homage in order to achieve peace. According to the contemporary Philippe de Mézières Richard had a personal dislike for war. Tuck suggests a more political motive behind his actions, arguing that Richard saw peace as a way of removing 'the opportunities which the Crown's financial weakness offered to its political opponents'.[114] Exactly what kind of peace Richard envisaged is less easy to discover.

English policies between cessation of hostilities in 1389 and the 28-year truce agreed in March 1396 have been the subject of recent discussion. Much of the debate revolves around the life grant of the duchy of Aquitaine to John of Gaunt, duke of Lancaster, on 2 March 1390.[115] Although this was made with the approval of parliament, it stated that Gaunt should hold the duchy of Richard as king of *France*. This appears to be a major shift from the Brétigny position which gave sovereignty over an enlarged Aquitaine to the king of *England*. Palmer interpreted the grant as the first stage in a proposed peace settlement to which Richard was wholeheartedly committed: Richard would renounce his claim to the French throne and his right to sovereignty in return for Gaunt's holding Aquitaine of the French king. For Palmer, this was the basis upon which peace was pursued between 1390 and 1394, and was the logical conclusion of the proposals made in the 1370s and 80s that the duchy should be vested in someone other than the king of England.[116] In June 1393 two English dukes (Lancaster and his youngest brother Gloucester) and two French dukes (Berry and Burgundy) seem to have agreed on terms: that French sovereignty over the duchy (restored approximately to its 1360 boundaries) should be accepted, whilst the tenure of Calais and La Rochelle should be deferred to a meeting of the two kings. In this agreement, Gaunt was to continue to hold the duchy for life and was to pay homage to the French king for its *usufruct*. Richard was to pay liege homage to the French king for the *propriété* of the duchy, although there was to be further discussion on how the *ressort* and sovereignty could be modified to avoid the threat of confiscation and war in the future.[117] Palmer suggests that this agreement was then confirmed by a secret, but now lost, treaty between Richard II and Charles VI. These terms, however, never formed the basis of a full peace settlement. Palmer explains that when Gaunt arrived in the duchy in 1394, the Gascons refused to accept his authority: they feared that Richard would agree to his holding the duchy of the French king and that it would be irrevocably alienated from the English crown contrary to previous custom and to their wishes. As a result, Richard was forced to reassure the Gascons by recalling Gaunt, by resuming royal control over the duchy and by dropping the plans of 1393.[118]

Palmer's interpretation has been much criticised. Vale accused him of conflating the negotiations of 1390 and those of 1393–4, reminding us that at the earlier date all Richard was prepared to discuss was the *possibility* of one of his sons (yet to be born) holding the duchy from Charles VI in simple homage. Vale suggested that there was no settled English peace policy in the 1390s let alone in the 1370s and 80s.[119] He considered that Gaunt's unpopularity in the duchy stemmed partly from his interference in local issues. Moreover, Richard reassured the Gascons that the grant to Gaunt had not been intended to diminish his own sovereignty or make any changes to the status of the duchy.[120] Tuck has subsequently suggested that a more serious stumbling block was the reaction of parliament (as recorded in the Roll of Parliament and in the *Westminster Chronicle*) when the 1393 terms were put before it in January 1394.[121] Tuck's interpretation is that parliament considered the payment of liege homage unacceptable, but that simple homage could be paid so long as it was modified to avoid the pitfalls of the pre-1337 position. He concludes that 'faced with the rejection by parliament of a crucial part of the draft agreement, Richard and John of Gaunt now abandoned the attempt to conclude a final peace with France'. Phillpotts has recently advanced a different interpretation.[122] He considers the whole plan to have been Gaunt's rather than Richard's. Having given up his Castilian claim, Gaunt had 'fixed upon Guyenne as his prospective principality, envisaging himself as the semi-independent ruler of an enlarged duchy', but also as 'the governing mentor of his nephew's kingdom', and possibly 'the natural successor to the childless Richard's English throne and French claims'. Gaunt thus colluded in 1393 with what the French dukes wanted. By 1395, however, Richard had withdrawn his support for Gaunt's plans, perhaps because of opposition in Gascony and England, the latter evidenced as much by the Cheshire revolt of 1393 as by the parliament of January 1394.

It is unlikely that the debate will end there, because many features of the period 1390–6 remain obscure. The attitude of Richard II is complex. He appears at first sight to have been committed to peace and even willing to give up his French title, but there is no conclusive evidence that he wanted to overturn the basic principles of Brétigny. He did not enter into discussions over the modifications of sovereignty or over the tenure of Calais as the 1393 terms had demanded. His grant of the duchy to Gaunt may not have been intended as the prelude to the surrender of sovereignty to the French king. Indeed Phillpotts has suggested that by using the title king of France in the grant to Gaunt, Richard may have been emphasising his claim to the throne by creating an appanage for a member of his family in what was explicitly French royal fashion.[123] The grant reveals, however, an inherent contradiction between the claim to the French throne and the claim to Brétigny-style full sovereignty. Since the readoption of the title king of France in 1369 it had not been entirely clear whether the English kings held their French possessions as kings of France or as kings of England. Edward III certainly abandoned his title 'lord of Aquitaine' when he resumed the kingship of France. In subsequent administration of the overseas lands both he and his grandson used both of their royal titles. In practice this made little difference since the lands were still considered, both by the Gascons and themselves, as theirs in full sovereignty, as the Brétigny/Calais settlement had established. Only when the grant to Gaunt necessitated the closer definition of these matters were they brought into focus. Richard seems to have been in a dilemma, wanting to reassure the Gascons yet without seeming to limit his uncle's authority or his own sovereignty in the area.[124] Richard's relationship with Gaunt is also difficult to assess. It is hard to believe that the king who had reasserted his authority in 1389 without his uncle's help would then sit back and let him dictate foreign policy. Yet that is clearly what contemporaries thought. Gaunt's unpopularity in the early 1390s stemmed from his French ambitions which, the *Westminster Chronicle* suggests, would have been treasonable if held by lesser men. The *Eulogium Historiarum*, albeit a rather problematic source, adds that Gaunt told the parliament that there was no value in keeping the French royal title, and that Calais cost more than it was worth.[125]

Yet is it credible that Gaunt's plans were not also those of Richard? We must assume that Richard had given Gaunt power to negotiate in 1393. The parliament roll of January 1394 suggests, however, that it was the *king* and the Lords, not the Commons, who objected to the payment of liege homage and who wanted changes to the terms of simple homage, so that even at this stage Richard seems to have been expressing his disagreement with Gaunt's plans. It is also interesting that there is no mention of Gaunt as holder of the duchy in these parliamentary discussions. There is no proof, beyond a comment in Froissart's *Chroniques*, that Richard gave Gaunt the duchy in hereditary tenure in 1394, or that he saw the latter as his royal heir.[126] Neither is it clear what role Gloucester played, for whilst he appears to have been keen on peace as he and his brother had negotiated it in 1393, four years later he was criticising the king's decision to withdraw from Brest and Cherbourg.[127] Various factors seem to have combined over the course of 1394 and 1395 to persuade Richard to drop the 1393 plans, if indeed he had ever been keen on them, and to pursue a different line apparently on his own initiative. No doubt these included reactions in England and Gascony, but perhaps a more important factor, as Palmer notes too, was the death of the queen, Anne of Bohemia, on 7 June 1394.[128] Richard's decision in March 1395 to seek the hand of Yolande of Aragon was scarcely the move of someone anxious to secure peace with France. Alarmed by this proposal and by the threat of a revival of English interest in Spain, the French made approaches in May 1395 for a marriage to Charles VI's six-year-old daughter, Isabella. Richard's response was to demand the full Brétigny terms plus Normandy, Anjou and

Maine for the sons of the marriage.[129] This may have been excessive, but it is clear that the English now had the upper hand in negotiations, undoubtedly because of changing political circumstances in France caused by the growing insanity of Charles VI since 1392. The French were by no means as strong or united in 1396 as they had been in 1393. Whoever Richard married, the prospect of his having direct heirs once and for all ended the chances of Gaunt's line possessing Gascony in perpetuity.

In the 28-year truce of 9 March 1396 which preserved the status quo, Richard came to a less disadvantageous settlement than that proposed in 1393.[130] He preserved all his claims intact: he could still call himself king of France, retain rights to all the Brétigny lands, and rule his existing possessions in full sovereignty, thereby reassuring the Gascons. The lengthy cessation of war (effectively to March 1426 as there were still two years of the existing truce to run) would remove the need for heavy war taxation. He could also enjoy Isabella's dowry of £133,333 and subsequently gained the prospect of her father's aid against his domestic enemies. The fall in war expenditure against the French enabled him to launch a campaign into Ireland. From 1396 Richard exercised greater authority than ever before at home and clearly sought to cut a larger figure on the European stage as a whole.[131]

The settlement gave rise to two unique events. One was the first Anglo-French royal marriage since 1308. The other, which occurred on 28 October 1396, was the first meeting of the two kings on equal terms since 1331. The heat had been taken out of the issues. Richard's retention of the French royal title kept his options open, giving him the potential of renewing his involvement in France. But in immediate, practical terms his use of the French title was meaningless. Four Valois kings had survived the Plantagenet challenge, and now the meeting and marriage implied Richard's recognition of Charles as king of France – an appellation that is found in some documents from 1397 to 1399.[132] During the long cessation of hostilities, the French could continue to rule as part of their kingdom the lands lost in 1360 but subsequently recovered; the English could enjoy *de facto* sovereign possession of what remained in their hands in Gascony and Calais and had not been forced to agree to any limitations on this sovereignty. In the first years of the truce neither side seems to have been interested in negotiating a full peace settlement. Nor, however, did they do much to threaten Anglo-French rapprochement. For them the truce was an adequate resolution of their disputes – disputes which the last 60 years had shown to be basically insoluble. It might have run its course had Richard remained king, and time might well have legitimised the status quo which it maintained. By September 1399, however, Richard had been deposed, France was sliding towards civil war and hopes of Anglo-French reconciliation were once more shattered.

3

NEW WARS OR OLD? ANGLO-FRENCH CONFLICT IN THE FIFTEENTH CENTURY

The Reign of Henry IV (1399–1413)

Henry IV's reign can easily be dismissed as insignificant in terms of English activities in France, particularly as it lacks the flamboyance and decisiveness of that of his son, Henry V (1413–22). As we shall see, however, the policies of the father prepared the way for the actions of the son. More importantly, perhaps, they preserved English interests in France at a time when they could well have foundered.

The deposition of Richard II in September 1399 by his cousin, Henry Bolingbroke, son of John of Gaunt, is of considerable importance in Anglo-French relations. Whether Richard's deposition was in part occasioned by opposition to the truce has never been firmly established. His 'peace policy' was not one of the charges made against him in the deposition articles. What was more at issue in England, perhaps, was his tendency towards autocratic rule which the cessation of hostilities with France had facilitated. Even so, two French chroniclers reported that on his return from exile Bolingbroke circulated letters claiming that Richard was planning to sell off all the possessions in France just as he had disposed of Brest and Cherbourg.[1] In terms of Anglo-French relations, any change of ruler was bound to have some impact, but that of 1399 had extra significance because it was a usurpation. The French never formally recognised Henry IV's kingship of England, and in 1405 went so far as to send military aid to the Welsh rebels.[2] Henry's hold on the English throne was not totally secure until 1408. But the French monarchy was also in disarray. Charles VI had shown the first signs of madness in 1392, but over the first decade of the fifteenth century his condition seems to have deteriorated – Froissart even ascribes this to the king's hearing of his son-in-law's deposition.[3] Charles's incapacity exacerbated the struggle for control of government, so that by 1410 France had been plunged into fully-fledged civil war between the Orléanist (or Armagnac) and Burgundian factions.

Following the deposition, the French initially pursued a hostile line, hoping to persuade the Gascons to drop their English allegiance. Despite the legacy of hostility to Gaunt's rule, however, the duchy accepted his son as king.[4] Once Richard's death was known, French policies were constrained by the need to ensure the safe return of Isabella. Pistono suggests that this persuaded Charles to confirm the truce on 31 January 1400.[5] As for Henry, one might assume that, as a usurper, he would have been ill-advised to stir up conflict with France. Yet in the face of initial French hostility and the continuing refusal to recognise him as king, he drew back from confirming the truce immediately. It seems that neither side knew exactly what its policy should be. As a result there was much posturing. Henry blew hot and cold over the possibility of Isabella's marriage to one of his own sons and equivocated over the return of both her and her dowry. Even when he finally expressed his willingness to confirm the truce in May 1400, Anglo-French relations remained delicate. In the following year, the French threatened invasion of Gascony. In response the English council discussed the prospect of war, but some lords were unenthusiastic because of the financial implications.[6] Indeed, shortage of resources continued to form a major constraint on Henry's policies towards France.

By 1402, with Isabella safely back home, the French once more moved onto the offensive. Because of the complex state of

French politics, this came in the form of individual rather than official action, and the state of truce between England and France was never formally rescinded. Over the next four years, Orléans – who may well have assisted Henry's return to England in 1399 – forsook his erstwhile ally and launched attacks on lands in Gascony which bordered his own possessions. The count of St Pol, married to Richard II's half-sister, raided the coasts of England and Gascony, and both he and the duke of Burgundy threatened Calais.[7] Between 1404 and 1406, the English were seriously threatened on land and sea, and were desperately short of cash. The seriousness of the situation must be acknowledged, for it coincided with resistance to Henry in England and with expensive campaigns in Wales. Henry was also outmanoeuvred in his attempts to gain influence in Brittany; despite his marriage to John IV's widow, control of the duke's heir fell to the duke of Burgundy. There was perhaps a real threat that Gascony would be lost. Yet it was not, and herein lies the significance of Henry's reign. Enough Gascons remained loyal; Henry had been astute in appointing, unusually, a Gascon-born seneschal. He also dispatched sufficient troops, although never fulfilling his intention of leading them himself, presumably because of fears of what might happen if he left England. None of the problems was really solved, but Orléans' failure to take the key town of Bourg in January 1407 and his murder in the following November removed the principal threat in Gascony.[8] In March 1407, the signing of a mercantile truce with the duke of Burgundy as ruler of Flanders lessened the threat to Calais and the Channel, although fears of his hostile intentions remained.[9]

Henry took the defence of his French possessions seriously but his policies had been determined so far by the need to respond to French aggression. Two further aspects of his reign need consideration. The first is his stance on the claim to the French throne and on the status of his French lands. The second is his response to changing political circumstances in France, which led to the launching of English expeditions in 1411 and 1412.

With respect to the first, Henry seems to have been in some confusion over his French royal title. He did not hesitate to take it up in 1399. Indeed, thoughts of the French title may have been one reason for abandoning the initial policy of claiming the English throne by his maternal rather than paternal descent. Advisers soon told him there was no truth in the rumour that his mother's ancestor, Edmund Crouchback, had been the first-born son of Henry III, put aside because of deformity; but to have held his English title by such means could perhaps have undermined his claim to the French throne, which was only his by direct descent from Edward III. Consideration for the French title may also have led to the abandonment of his plan of June 1406 to restrict the succession of the English and French crowns and to 'all other lordships on the other side of the sea' to the male line. This would have cast doubts on the French claim which came through a woman, although it would have benefited Henry by excluding rivals for the English throne whose claims of descent from the second, rather than the third, son of Edward III were through the female line.[10]

On the whole, however, it is difficult to deny Perroy's conclusion that in this period the French title was 'one of England's stage properties'.[11] Henry had no watertight right to either of his royal crowns: it can thus be suggested that the French title was no longer held by inheritance but was merely an appendage of the crown of England, much as it was to be in later centuries. Although Henry never announced his willingness to surrender the title, he was negotiating in March 1409 for the marriage of his eldest son to Charles's daughter Catherine 'or some other woman of the royal blood of France', thereby implicitly admitting that France had its own king.[12] Yet the title had to be held to legitimise Henry as king of England and as Richard II's rightful successor. A sense of honour also demanded that it should be retained, even if it meant little to its holder.

Henry's attitude to Calais and Gascony was quite different. He followed the belief that the Treaty of Brétigny still stood, and that these lands were the property of the English crown inalienably and in full sovereignty. On 23 October 1399 he named his eldest son (the future Henry V) as duke of Aquitaine.[13] The prince did not pay homage for the duchy, as he had done for his English lands; its administration continued to be conducted in the name of the king. The title was granted to emphasise

Henry IV's commitment to the duchy's inalienability from the crown, to reassure the Gascons who had been so perturbed by the grant to Gaunt. Not surprisingly, Henry was greatly displeased by the creation of the Dauphin as duke of Guienne in 1402 because this was an obvious denial of English rights by Brétigny, let alone of the terms of the 1396 truce. English commitment to a fully sovereign Gascony persisted. In the parliament of 1410, the notion that the duchy was annexed to the crown of England was restated, and in February 1412 the inhabitants of the duchy were again confirmed as the subjects of Henry as king of England.[14]

The difference in Henry's attitudes to his lands and to the claim upon the throne of France is well evidenced by military involvement there towards the end of his reign, once he was secure in his English kingship. By 1410 there was outright civil war between the parties of Burgundy and Orléans: the threat to England and Gascony thus diminished. The warring factions turned to the English king for assistance. During Henry's illness in 1411, Prince Henry chose to send a small company to the duke of Burgundy, possibly in return for a promise of assistance in the recovery of Normandy.[15] If true, this is a significant anticipation of where his interests were to lie as king. Back in control of the government in January 1412, King Henry was approached by the dukes of Orléans, Berry, Bourbon and Alençon, offering the restitution of the duchy of Aquitaine 'to the king of England as his by hereditary right'. In the Treaty of Bourges of 18 May 1412, they confirmed that Henry should have the duchy 'completely and in as full liberty as his ducal predecessors', and even agreed that lands in their possession which had been part of the Brétigny settlement should be returned at their deaths to the English king, to whom homage would be paid in the meantime. In return Henry agreed not to aid the Burgundians.[16] In fact he went further than that. On 8 June he indented with his second son, Thomas, duke of Clarence, to take 4000 men to the aid of the dukes.[17] After disembarking at Edward III's landing place of St Vaast La Hougue in mid-August, Clarence passed through Maine and Anjou intending to meet with the dukes' army at Blois. In the event, Burgundy made peace with his enemies before Clarence arrived so that the dukes' promises to Henry IV were never fulfilled.

The whole incident could be dismissed as mere mercenary service, particularly as, after the first three months of Exchequer pay, Clarence's men were to be financed by the French dukes. There has been debate over whether Henry was duped by the dukes into providing troops when there was little realistic hope of their aid for his cause; after all, the duchy of Aquitaine was not theirs to bestow, nor did they control Charles VI's government at this juncture. None the less, the incident was of great significance. Henry's acceptance of the offer (where the dukes called him king of England and duke of Aquitaine) was tantamount to his abandoning the French royal title. Although in practice he never did so, he had gone further towards this end than any king since Edward III in the Brétigny settlement. Moreover, the gravity of political divisions in France had been revealed. Henry IV, like his son later, saw the potential this gave to English interests. The French monarchy was at its lowest ebb. By 1413 the Lancastrian dynasty was well established and had managed to maintain virtually intact the French possessions it had acquired with the English crown in 1399. Additionally, the English military community had already shown its willingness to go to war against the French. Had Henry IV lived longer he might well have exploited French divisions further instead of having to leave it to his son to do so.[18]

Henry V and the Conquest of Normandy

Henry V's policy of intervention was the logical continuation of Henry IV's last campaign. But certain contrasts must be pointed out. Henry IV was invited in: Henry V was not. The latter invaded in 1415 and 1417 in pursuit of his own quarrel, not the quarrel of others. Nor was he fortified by alliances. He might have hoped for Burgundian collusion but there is no conclusive evidence of an agreement before the end of 1419. Until that point, Henry's actions were as much anti-Burgundian as anti-Orléanist, particularly as Normandy was partly under Burgundian control when Henry invaded. There are several other ways in which Henry's wars are unique. From 1417 he was intent upon systematic conquest of territory – that is, Normandy – in a way that none of his predecessors had been. Moreover, no king since Richard I had been absent so continuously on campaign as Henry was between 1417 and 1421. A bare five years from his first invasion, Henry forced the French to come to a negotiated settlement. Not only was this a speedier agreement than any of his predecessors had managed but also the settlement appeared to give more than any other had done. The Treaty of Troyes (24 May 1420) made Henry heir and regent of Charles VI, and gave him control, in theory, of the whole of France. As a final point of contrast with Edward III and Henry VI at least, Henry had the fortune to die in victory rather than defeat.

All of this uniqueness does not make Henry's initial war aims any easier to ascertain. As Le Patourel pointed out, 'it cannot be argued that [Edward III's] claim to the throne of France had never been serious because it was given up in his name at Brétigny'.[19] Likewise, just because Henry V came close to gaining the French crown by virtue of the treaty of 1420 it cannot be assumed that the crown was his aim all along. It is easy to fall into the trap of accepting that Henry was bent on war right from his accession and that his early diplomatic moves were merely preparatory to conflict: this interpretation depends on the notion that he deliberately set his demands high so that the French would reject them, thereby justifying his recourse to arms. What seems equally likely is that he wanted to achieve a settlement at a time when the French were weak. To this end he was prepared to try various 'ways', as his diplomatic documents describe, until war appeared the best option. He had already shown a keen interest in French affairs in his father's reign; by virtue both of personal inclination and of the opportunities which arose, he was able to go further than Henry IV in diplomacy and in warfare.

Henry's policy is revealed by his decision to send an embassy to Paris in August 1414, which marks the first serious attempt to negotiate on the territorial issues since the early 1390s. Right at the outset the embassy 'condescended' to drop the claim to the throne in favour of a territorial settlement, which is a clear indication of Henry's priorities, as too is his commissioning of materials concerning the Treaty of Brétigny and the 1412 agreement.[20] There can be no doubt, too, that he was committed to a marriage with Catherine, the youngest daughter of Charles VI. He had already promised in January 1414 to marry no one else, and the marriage remained a constant demand until effected in June 1420. Both sides were keen on the match: it is difficult to see why else both Henry and Catherine remained unmarried. That did not, of course, prevent haggling over the level of dowry. Henry's territorial demands in 1414 were steep: the restitution in full sovereignty of all the lands of Brétigny, plus the similar tenure of Normandy, Touraine, Maine and Anjou, along with the homage of Brittany and Flanders and the payment of 1.6 million *écus* still owing from John II's ransom. To these he added new demands for the castles of Beaufort and Nogent as well as the moiety of Provence. This was an interesting allusion to his Lancastrian pedigree since his claim stemmed from the fact that they had been the inheritance of the second wife of Edmund Crouchback, brother of Edward I and first earl of Lancaster. His demands may seem unrealistic – they were, after all, an opening bid – but the French immediately declared themselves ready to restore the duchy of Aquitaine. In the context of Anglo-French negotiations of the Hundred Years War, this was a substantial offer. Its similarity to that of 1412 is not surprising given that the same group of dukes now controlled Charles VI's government. It reveals their continuing fear of an Anglo-Burgundian alliance.

Henry refused this offer, speculating perhaps that further civil war in France might bring greater gains, and hoping for Burgundian aid. This was a miscalculation, for by the time of his second embassy in February 1415, Burgundy and Orléans had been reconciled. Despite frequent negotiations over the course of 1414, Henry had failed to commit Burgundy to his support. Perhaps in the knowledge of this, Henry reduced his demands in his second embassy effectively to the terms of the 'great peace' of Brétigny, dropping his claim to lands north of the Loire and offering to accept a lower dowry.[21] But now that the civil war was in temporary abeyance, the French could afford to be uncooperative. They thus reduced their offer to certain lands in Aquitaine to be held as fiefs, a cancellation of John's ransom in its entirety, and an unacceptably low dowry. It was in the face of this that Henry began serious preparations for war – a risk perhaps whilst the French were united, but a reaction very much prompted by French intransigence. Much is made of Henry's desire for war but we must not forget that in 1415 the French were equally if not more bellicose. They clearly thought little of the English military threat: after all, they were able to field at least twice as many men at Agincourt, and until the battle they limited English freedom of action considerably. Not surprisingly, therefore, the embassy which they sent in June 1415 was anxious merely to make the French appear the wronged party. In a splendid example of a war of words, the archbishop of Rouen denied Henry's right even to the English throne – a challenge to which Henry responded by issuing an ultimatum that he would commence the conquest of France if Aquitaine, Poitou, Normandy, Maine, Anjou, Touraine and Ponthieu were not surrendered to him in full sovereignty.[22]

It is not clear when Henry decided upon a Norman landing. His first thought may have been to campaign in Gascony. That is a destination given in some of the early contracts of recruitment (April 1415), although it is usually supposed that this, and the decision to embark from Southampton, was a smokescreen for an invasion of Normandy to which he was already committed.[23] Logistically, an attack on the north was easier, particularly when there were over 10,000 men to transport. He may have been encouraged by the fact that some of the Norman garrisons were in Burgundian hands, although in practice this seems to have made little difference to the level of resistance offered. The siege of Harfleur (19 August–23 September 1415) shows that Henry wanted to establish a bridgehead which could be revictualled by sea and could provide a base for further expansion. There is no definite indication that he had hoped from the start to do battle against the French. The size of his army, the arrangements for provisioning and the fact that the indentures specified a year's service suggest that he intended to make conquests in Normandy, perhaps by dividing his army as in the 1417 campaign, or by carrying out a lengthy *chevauchée*, possibly towards Bordeaux. Neither was to happen. The siege of Harfleur saw his army depleted by sickness and desertion. In addition he had to install a large garrison to defend the town. Immediately after the surrender he seems to have decided to take the rest of his army (now perhaps at two-thirds of its initial strength) to Calais by the quickest route; there were no further attempts to make conquests.[24] He took a considerable gamble in giving battle on 25 October. His army was exhausted by its tortuous march northwards. The French, on the other hand, were fresher and in much larger numbers. Henry was very lucky or very skilful, depending upon one's perspective, to win the day and thus to return to England in triumph in mid-November, the campaign having lasted only three months out of the proposed twelve.

The impact of Agincourt parallels that of Crécy. The defeat hardened French attitudes so that, much as in the late 1340s, they refused to contemplate negotiations with England or to accept the Emperor Sigismund's mediation. They were determined to recover Harfleur: the English ability to defend it is perhaps as significant as their success at Agincourt. As after Crécy, too, the French were demoralised and humiliated. Many French nobles had been killed; others, including the duke of Orléans and many of his faction, were prisoners in England. Burgundy had chosen to absent himself from the battle, although some of his party participated. Now he strove to fill the power vacuum which the battle had created in France. Henry had shown the seriousness of his intentions by raising the largest army since 1359, even if the crown jewels had been mortgaged, as in 1338–40, to pay its wages. By his victory, Henry put the English star into the ascendant for the first time since the 1360s. His success could serve only to increase English enthusiasm for, and willingness to finance, further war.

Between the landing of his second campaign at the mouth of the River Touque on 1 August 1417 and the murder of the duke of Burgundy on 10 September 1419, Henry's military and diplomatic activities reveal his principal objective to be the conquest of Normandy. It is also clear that he hoped, by military pressure, to force the French to accept his sovereign rule there and in the Brétigny lands. Henry's second campaign was unprecedented. This was a new kind of war. Never had there been such a sustained effort to conquer and garrison a large expanse of enemy territory. Fourteenth-century *chevauchées* had led to few, if any, places being retained in English hands. Some garrisons had been maintained in Aquitaine, Brittany and Normandy but never on as extensive or official a scale. Henry's conquest compares most closely with Edward's capture of Calais. Both combined the systematic occupation of territory with colonisation. Henry had already started to make land grants after the capture of Harfleur, expelling some of the native population as Edward had done at Calais. Almost as soon as he landed on his second campaign, he started to distribute lands to soldiers and administrators.[25] This policy continued throughout the occupation of the duchy, being adopted too in other areas of northern France which fell under English control. It extended royal powers of patronage as well as giving a vested interest in the war to men of all ranks, from the noble who gained an entire duchy or county to the archer who received a few pounds in rent on a house or smallholding. This land distribution was at the expense of the native population and in some ways ran counter to Henry's growing efforts to be accepted as legitimate ruler of Normandy.[26]

Henry's policy towards the Normans is of great interest. Like Edward III he adopted the title duke of Normandy, although using it alongside his French royal title as his predecessor had also done. This may have been an appeal to feelings of separatism although it has never been established whether Normandy – an integral part of the French royal domains since 1204 – was particularly separatist at this point. Certainly most of its nobility did not accept English rule. If Henry was to hope for the duchy in full sovereignty, however, it was in his interests to emulate his ducal ancestors, who had been largely independent of French royal control. This was certainly implied in Thomas Walsingham's *Ypodigma Neustriae* (c.1419), which took as its starting point the first duke, Rollo.[27] When Caen was taken in September 1418, mention was made of its ancient loyalties as the capital of the Norman dukes. Following the surrender of Rouen early in the next year, Henry not only wore the Norman ducal robes but also revived some ancient institutions.[28] Significantly, too, he had already sought to establish a form of feudal tenure in the duchy, although its links with the past are uncertain.[29] The ducal title was used from at least November 1417 although it does not appear in all documents. Henry seems to have dropped it in the summer of 1419, although this does not prove that the crown had then become his main objective.[30]

The Norman campaign was maintained uninterruptedly for more than two years and is perhaps the longest continuous English action of the entire Hundred Years War.[31] There were some lengthy sieges, the most notorious being that of Rouen (30 July 1418–19 January 1419) but, once the major places had fallen, the rest tended to offer no resistance. The lack of opposition is partly related to English success and partly to continuing conflicts within France. Duke John of Burgundy had finally managed to seize control of the government in May 1418. A French civil war was now being waged alongside the Anglo-French conflict, with the Dauphin Charles, fleeing southwards, becoming the focus of opposition to the Burgundians.

Henry attempted to exploit this division, entering into separate negotiations with the representatives of the king and Burgundy, and of the Dauphin. What is most significant is that his demands continued to focus on territory and a marriage with Catherine rather than on the French throne. By June 1419, Normandy was almost all his: he had begun to move into neighbouring areas to the east, lands which he was to term the 'pays de conquête'. There is a strong possibility that at this stage an agreement was nearly reached with the royal/Burgundian group at Meulan.[32] Full details are not known but it most likely embodied the Brétigny terms plus Normandy in full sovereignty. In return Henry would drop his French title and his demands for Touraine, Maine, Anjou and Montreuil in Ponthieu. The size of Catherine's dowry was still causing debate. But attention was now being paid to the lesser issues such as the restitution of ecclesiastical and secular lands in Normandy and the maintenance of the privileges of the Universities – considerations which make it likely that the major issues had been settled. Like Edward III before him, Henry's military success was forcing the French to make concessions even of lands which were not in his possession.

We cannot be certain that Henry would have ended his attack there. What was perhaps most significant in preventing the ratification of this agreement was the reconciliation of the Dauphin and the duke of Burgundy in mid-July, whereby they agreed to act together to drive out the English.[33] The proposed sell-out to the English at Meulan had apparently caused consternation in the Burgundian camp. As a Parisian chronicler notes, 'it would be very hard for the King of France, who ought to be sovereign king amongst all Christians, to be forced to obey his ancient mortal enemy because he was at variance with his son'.[34] Henry certainly feared the prospect of French unity, particularly in the light of additional Scottish and Castilian aid to the Dauphin at this point. None the less, his response was characteristically forceful; he stormed Pontoise on 30 July and began to threaten Paris itself, which was increasingly short of food. He did not, however, close the door on negotiations, although he now added Pontoise and subsequently the whole Vexin to his demands.[35]

We shall never know whether Henry would have been able to take Paris by force, or indeed whether he would have tried to do so, for on 10 September Duke John of Burgundy was murdered by the Dauphin's men on the bridge at Montereau, 45 miles to the south-east of the capital. Chroniclers suggest that John's heir, Philip, immediately sought rapprochement with Henry, and thus arose the agreement finally embodied in the Treaty of Troyes whereby Henry became heir and Regent to Charles VI.[36] Bonenfant's detailed study of the diplomatic documents of this period shows that in fact Henry himself and the government in Paris played the major roles in bringing about such a settlement.[37] On 19 September the royal council in Paris sent an embassy to Henry at Gisors in the hope of gaining a truce to save Paris, but also to negotiate vengeance for the murder.[38] Henry's reply of 27 September makes the first mention of terms which later formed the basis of the treaty.[39]

Henry now restated his claim to the throne in a more forthright and practical manner than ever before, suggesting that he should take the crown at the death of Charles VI. This was a real claim, not a bargaining counter. Henry had responded quickly to the new opportunities offered. The claim was accompanied by the offer of marriage to Catherine without dowry (a very significant sign of Henry's seriousness), the proposal for his effective adoption by Charles, and the proviso that the kingdoms of England and France should not be subject to each other. Charles VI's council appears to have been stupefied, claiming that Henry's demands at Meulan had been nothing like this. Henry replied that now things were different ('les choses sont autres').[40] His embassy also made it quite clear that although he was prepared to come to an alliance with the Duke Philip of Burgundy, his own claim to the throne was to take precedence over that of the duke. Indeed, Henry's speed in putting forward his claim may have been to forestall any attempts to make Philip heir. It is significant that around this time Henry tightened the arrangements for the safekeeping in England of the duke of Orléans, for unless the rules of succession were changed, the latter would be heir presumptive in the event of the Dauphin's disinheritance for implication in the murder of Duke John.[41]

Henry had clearly set his sights on the throne, but was astute enough to refuse a truce until negotiations had proceeded further and his latest target, Meulan, had fallen into his hands. The young and inexperienced Duke Philip was still hoping for a territorial settlement, but Henry stood firm throughout all the complicated manoeuvrings of October and November, threatening an attack on Paris if his demands were not met.[42] By 2 December Philip had accepted Henry's terms in return for a promise of aid in avenging his father's murder.[43] By early February, the city of Paris and the king and queen at Troyes had given their approval, after rejecting the Dauphin's approaches, and in April the Estates added their consent.[44] After envoys had finalised detailed terms, Henry met Charles VI and Philip at Troyes on 20 May, and the treaty was ratified the next day.[45] At the same time Henry was betrothed to Catherine and their wedding was celebrated on 2 June. Henry was now heir as well as Regent of the king of France. But he could no longer claim to be king of France himself.

The Treaty of Troyes

The treaty is a lengthy and complex document which cannot be
fully discussed here, so we shall concentrate only on those
clauses which relate to themes which have occupied this book to
date, namely the claim to the French throne and the territorial
dimensions. In all respects, the treaty marks a major turning
point in Anglo-French relations. It was the first full peace since
1360 and thus technically ended the hostilities which had persisted since 1369. It created peace between the two nations by
the prospect of their having the same ruler. It was a very different settlement from any previous agreement, and as we shall
see, it created as many problems as it solved.

On the question of the French throne, the treaty appears clear
cut. In clause 2, the right of Charles to remain king for the rest of
his lifetime was assured. At his death, and thenceforward, the
crown of France was to be held by Henry and his heirs. In the
interim, given Charles's mental incapacity, Henry was to be
Regent. But several complexities immediately surface. By becoming Charles's heir, Henry was in practice abandoning his
claim to the French throne through his descent from Edward
III, and recognising for the first time Charles's right to be king.
The treaty was thus made by Henry named not as king of
England and France but as king of England, heir and Regent of
France and lord of Ireland. No mention was made of his previous claim to the crown, or of its renunciation. Henry's right
now derived from the terms of the treaty. It did not derive from
his marriage to Catherine, which was made 'for the good of the
peace'. Although the treaty stated that by the marriage 'Charles
and Isabel are made our father and mother', this was not the
means by which Henry became heir, for that would have been
tantamount to admitting Catherine's own rights of transmission.
Thus the treaty did not restrict Henry's heirs to his issue by
Catherine. The crucial clause was 24, where it was stated that
the kingdoms of France and England should always be ruled by
one person 'and not divided under different kings'. In theory,
therefore, whoever was Henry's heir to the English throne,
whether his child or a member of the collateral lines of his

family, would also be king of France. It is interesting to speculate what would have happened if Henry and Catherine had produced only female offspring, given that the decision of 1406 to allow females to succeed in England still stood. There were thus potential weaknesses and causes of controversy in the most fundamental clauses of the treaty. It is not surprising that some French chroniclers thought the treaty permitted only the male heirs of the marriage to inherit the French throne, or that English writers continued to stress the claim through descent from Edward III, or else both by this means and by the treaty.[46]

As luck would have it, Henry and Catherine had only one child, a boy, who became king of England and heir of France at his father's death on 31 August 1422, and king of France at the death of Charles VI on the following 21 October. Had he lived, Henry V could perhaps have been accepted as king of France, given that he had been recognised by Charles VI as heir, had enjoyed some success as Regent and was seen, by some Frenchmen at least, as the only hope for an end to civil war. Henry VI was only nine months old at the death of his father so that his rule had to be through others, which was bound to cause problems, not least in defining the respective roles of the duke of Burgundy and of the English royal family.[47] Henry's youth delayed his French coronation, with disastrous consequences. As Reims had fallen to the Dauphin in 1429, he was able to enjoy a coronation in the traditional crowning place of the French kings. Henry VI had to make do with a ceremony in Paris on 16 December 1431.[48] He was the only king of England ever to be crowned king of France.

His title, and indeed the whole of the Treaty of Troyes, was undermined by the fact that a son of Charles VI still lived. The treaty already referred to him as the 'so-called' Dauphin, but did not explicitly exclude him or the collateral lines of the Valois from the succession. His disinheritance had already been anticipated in the months following the murder at Montereau, but it was formally achieved by a *lit de justice* (essentially a royal legal hearing) at the Paris *parlement* on 23 December 1420. Charles was not indicted by name in the proceedings, but after all had been judged guilty, he was summoned for sentencing on 3 January

1421. When, not surprisingly, he failed to appear, he was banished and declared incapable of succession.[49] This was an essential corollary of the treaty, which had already committed Henry to reduce to obedience those lands which held to the Dauphinist or Armagnac party. The method of disinheritance raised considerable criticism in France in 1420 and later. In 1435 it was considered illegal by the doctors of law at Bologna, a judgement which helped to persuade Philip of Burgundy to renounce his allegiance to the treaty and to accept Charles VII as king in the Treaty of Arras (21 September 1435).[50] In practice, the problematical question of the disinheritance arose not so much from flaws in the legal proceedings as from actual circumstances. Charles always remained in a strong enough position to challenge the decision against him. He was already accepted as king in much of central and south-eastern France, and was thus able to raise troops and also taxes which bought Scottish military aid in the 1420s.[51] Joan of Arc's lifting of the siege of Orléans in May 1429 boosted his fortunes in the north. By May 1436, he had been crowned at Reims, had gained the allegiance of the duke of Burgundy and had recovered Paris. Thenceforward, he was in practice king of France, for relatively little territory outside Gascony, Normandy and Maine, and even fewer French nobles, remained loyal to Henry VI. Arguably, no flaws in the legal argument would have been found if the Anglo-Burgundians had managed to defeat or assassinate the Dauphin soon after 1420. As we have seen on many occasions in this study, military action was always the eventual arbiter of rights. A claim to kingship was valid only if territory could be secured.

This brings us to the second aspect of the Treaty of Troyes, the territorial dimension. Three topics need discussion: Normandy, Gascony, and the rule of France as a whole.

Henry V appears to have been in something of a dilemma over Normandy. By the time of the treaty, the duchy was almost entirely in his hands and he did not wish to abandon it. Thus by virtue of clause 18, only when Henry became king were the duchy and the 'pays de conquête' to come under the jurisdiction of the French crown. The treaty said nothing about the status of the duchy in the meantime so that it remained under his direct rule, effectively in full sovereignty without homage to Charles VI. As far as we know, Henry never used the title duke of Normandy after the treaty, although it was perhaps inscribed on his tomb in Westminster Abbey. Henry was so confident of his inheritance of the French throne in 1420 that he did not feel it necessary to demand that Normandy should be permanently removed from France and established as a fully sovereign possession of the English crown.

Another interesting omission in the Treaty of Troyes is mention of Gascony. This could be taken as signifying that, unlike Normandy, it was to pass to the king of France immediately rather than to continue being held by Henry. Or else it could be interpreted as indicating that the French now tacitly accepted English claims to full sovereignty as accorded by the Brétigny settlement. In this scenario, Gascony (and likewise Calais, which is also not mentioned in the treaty) was no longer part of the kingdom of France but a personal possession of the king of England, just as Henry and his predecessors had claimed all along. Vale considers this second interpretation by far the more likely.[52] Gascony was still referred to as 'our duchy', although Henry never styled himself, either before or after the treaty, as either duke or lord, the title which Edward III had assumed in 1360. The seal of the duchy retained its three lions, but acquired no fleur de lys, which does imply that Henry's authority there after Troyes was not as heir and Regent of France but as king of England. Indeed only four days before the treaty was signed, his seneschal of Gascony announced the king's intention of reconquering the whole duchy. Yet oaths to the treaty were ordered to be taken in the duchy and documents issued after the accession of Henry VI cite both his royal titles. It remains unclear whether authority in Gascony emanated from the kingship of England or of France. This did not seem to matter to the crown or to the duchy's inhabitants once there was an effective dual monarchy. There was no real problem until French military pressure from the late 1430s enabled Charles VII's negotiators to insist once more on the vassalic status of the duchy, and the English to consider seriously a territorial settlement once again.

With regard to France as a whole, the treaty made Henry V

heir and Regent of Charles VI as king of the entire kingdom. But in 1400 not all of France accepted the treaty. Lyon proved so loyal to the Dauphin that it imprisoned the Parisian embassy bringing news of the treaty, and even in northern France there were some misgivings.[53] Henry hoped to secure loyalty by means of the oaths which clause 13 of the treaty demanded from the nobility, leading townsmen and royal officials. He also invited opponents to enter into his obedience. These tactics were repeated by his brother, John, duke of Bedford, as Regent of France for Henry VI.[54] In addition, it was hoped to increase the acceptability of the new regime by promising in the treaty the retention of French laws, customs and institutions, and the exercise of good government (cls 7, 8, 9, 10 and 11). It seems that Henry and his successors took these promises seriously. There was no real attempt to anglicise either the personnel or the procedures of the government of France, although military control was largely entrusted to Englishmen.[55] Initially at least, the relative peace of the new regime seemed preferable to the anarchy of the old. By the early 1430s, however, this had been shattered by Charles's military advance. Thenceforward, the areas of France which accepted the treaty found themselves once more at the mercy of war so that the English could no longer pose as the bringers of peace. Opinion began to turn against them, even in Normandy, so that by 1449–50 there were many who welcomed Charles VII as liberator.

The treaty (cl. 12) obliged Henry to reduce to obedience territories still loyal to the Dauphin. It was thus an unusual peace treaty because it required the continuance of war. The problem was that Henry had entered into an open-ended commitment. This may have seemed capable of fulfilment in 1420 since the English had enjoyed considerable military success to date. But Henry could never have conquered and garrisoned the whole of France with English troops and at English expense; there was already disquiet in parliament on this. He presupposed his task would be feasible because he would be able to draw upon the taxative and military resources of the French crown. The attack on Dauphinist lands was to be in the name of Charles VI, so that any resistance could be interpreted as treasonable activity against the undeniably legitimate French king. This is perhaps the most important aspect of the treaty. It transformed the conflict from a national to a civil war. No longer was it fought between the English king and the French king, or between their two nations. Henry was in many respects merely perpetuating the French civil war by adding his weight to the Burgundian party which had controlled Charles VI. Whilst Henry was alive the duke of Burgundy remained very much a junior partner, but it was already obvious that Henry was only accepted as heir and Regent in areas controlled by himself or by Burgundy. Burgundian military and political assistance was thus crucial but there was a substantial price to pay. Henry's association with Burgundy made all Armagnacs his enemy, even those who were not already supporters of the Dauphin. The characteristics of civil war only began to diminish after 1429 when the Anglo-Burgundian alliance faltered and Charles met with military success and coronation. After Duke Philip defected in 1435, the war was once more between the French and English nations and their rulers, with the added complication that both Charles VII and Henry VI were crowned kings of France.

Campaigns in the last two years of Henry V's life indicated just how difficult it would be to fulfil clause 12. Only after lengthy sieges did Meaux and Melun, towns relatively close to Paris, surrender. The advance southwards into Maine and Anjou ended with the defeat of his eldest brother, the duke of Clarence, at the battle of Baugé in March 1421. Moreover, Henry had relatively few of the great lords of France in his obedience, save Burgundy and his followers. Thus even whilst Charles VI was alive France was split into two 'nations', a Dauphinist south and a north where the treaty was accepted, although by no means universally. Even in Normandy there were pockets of resistance. By the time of his death (31 August 1422) Henry may already have come to realise the impossibility of winning the whole of France. Sources suggest that on his death-bed he advised the English to focus on Normandy. He may also have wished Burgundy to be given the Regency of France. He further urged both the preservation of the Burgundian alliance and the banning of all negotiations with the

Dauphin. This emphatically suggests that he did not wish his successor to abandon the right to the French throne which the Treaty of Troyes had bestowed.[56]

1422–1451

Henry V thus bequeathed a problematic legacy. By the terms of the treaty, his baby son became king of France at the death of Charles VI on 21 October 1422. Acceptance of Henry VI's title, however, relied on military might, necessitating the sending of reinforcements from England almost every year thenceforward as well as the maintenance of garrisons in English-held areas. The sense of occupation never disappeared. From the Treaty of Troyes to the Truce of Tours in May 1444, there was no cessation of hostilities. This marks, therefore, the longest continuous period ever of open warfare between English and French. The dual monarchy was to experience many difficulties, but perhaps the major problem was Henry VI himself. In the 1420s and 30s, he was too young to lead policy or troops. Once he came of age in 1436, he showed a singular lack of interest in his French crown despite being the only king of England to have experienced a French coronation. As we shall see, his policies in the 1440s led to the loss of almost all his French lands. What is perhaps more remarkable is that the English met with as much success as they did in northern France. In broad terms, the explanation lies in Charles VII's inability, until the mid-1440s, to overcome divisions within his court and to improve his military organisation. A significant factor, too, is the high level of English commitment to France, at least until the same date, as recent studies of the reign of Henry VI have shown.[57]

During Henry's minority policies were formulated by others. Henry VI's eldest uncle, John, duke of Bedford, acted as Regent of France from 1422 to 1430 and, after the king's coronation, as governor general until his death on 9 September 1435. On the whole he pursued a rather conservative line. Following his dead brother's advice, he tried to maintain Normandy's administrative independence but was forced to have the duchy reintegrated within France. Even so, his strategy concentrated on the securing of Normandy and northern France. (English control in Gascony was scarcely extended at all under Lancastrian rule.) This was not entirely out of choice; it was occasioned by the high level of resistance in areas under ostensible Anglo-Burgundian control, resistance heartened, it seems, by the death of Henry V. The vulnerability of the Anglo-Burgundian position is revealed by the location of campaigns in 1423 and 1424, which aimed at the recovery of Meulan on the Seine, Le Crotoy at the mouth of the Somme, Gaillon and Mont-Saint-Michel.[58] Despite several subsequent sieges Mont-Saint-Michel never fell to Henry VI and remained a considerable threat to south-western Normandy. There was also considerable Anglo-Burgundian activity in Champagne, the Vermandois and Tierache, a major victory being scored on 31 July 1423 at Cravant. The hinterland of Paris was slowly, but never entirely, secured. An even more significant battle was won by Bedford against the Dauphin's largely Scottish army at Verneuil on 16 August 1424, although the location of this shows just how far the enemy were still able to penetrate into Normandy. After Verneuil, Normandy was secure enough to allow its garrisons to be reduced and for the move southwards to recommence. Campaigns were thus launched into Maine in late 1424, 1425, 1426 and 1427, much to the benefit of Bedford, who had been granted Maine and Anjou in 1424 in anticipation of their conquest. Garrisons were established in Maine and lands distributed much as they had been in Normandy, although much less evidence survives for them than for the duchy. It was clearly Bedford's intention to advance into Anjou; the Norman estates voted taxation for this purpose in the summer of 1428.

In the event, however, a move was made instead against Orléans. It seems most likely that this alternative plan was formulated in England, perhaps by Bedford's younger brother, Humphrey, duke of Gloucester, in collusion with Thomas, earl of Salisbury. The latter led 2500 troops raised in England to join with 1600 men of the garrisons and retinues in France in an attempt to breach the Dauphin's Loire frontier. For the first time, Bedford lost control of strategy: previous reinforcements sent from England had been placed at his disposal. The incident should be seen in the context of the problems of Henry VI's minority. The need to depute the rule of both England and France led to effectively separate administrations in both countries. Whilst Bedford was technically in charge in both lands, he could not hope to exercise the same authority as a king could. As Keen has recently suggested, the gulf between the English in France and the English in England widened as the war continued, with increasingly damaging effects.[59] In theory, the Orléans campaign had made sense. By a decisive blow against the Dauphin, his challenge to the north could have been ended. Gloucester and Salisbury had been leading commanders under Henry V, Bedford's service had only really begun in 1421. It may well be that they considered their policy to be closer to the wishes of the dead king than was the conservative and, to them, excessively pro-Burgundian stance of Bedford. The campaign began well, and had Joan of Arc not succeeded in raising the siege of Orléans and defeating the retreating English at Patay (18 June 1429), the outcome of the war could have been very different.

Instead, Charles went on to conquer much of Champagne and the upper Seine valley, to be crowned at Reims and to threaten Paris. The attack on Orléans had already alienated Burgundy as it was a challenge to his supposed zone of influence. He now began to toy with accepting Charles as king, although the legacy of bitterness was so strong that a full defection did not take place until 1435. An immediate result of Joan's victories was that the English were forced onto the defensive. Never again did they hold as much land as was in their possession when Salisbury began to besiege Orléans. Even worse, French success had encouraged further resistance in Normandy and its environs.[60] The next few years were largely taken up with attempts to recover places•lost, such as Château Gaillard on the Seine and Louviers on the Eure, the latter lying in an area which was to prove exceedingly vulnerable thenceforward. Louviers was retaken with the aid of some of the c.5000-strong army which accompanied Henry VI for his coronation at Paris on 16 December 1431, an event which Charles's crowning at Reims had made essential.

There are dangers, however, in writing off the English at this point, as though the final expulsions of 1449–53 follow in direct line from the defeats of 1429. Admittedly, the English gained no major victories after 1429, and they were required to give considerable attention to the defence of Normandy, particularly along its southern and north-eastern frontiers. But they held steady in the early 1430s, assisted by divisions within Charles's party. The continuing level of commitment to the double monarchy is revealed by large and frequent reinforcements being sent from England, along with money to help finance the garrisons of the duchy. More significant perhaps were further signs of conflict between Bedford and the English council, although again these seem to have been satisfactorily resolved. Events following Bedford's death proved more difficult to deal with. The defection of Burgundy led to a threat to Calais in 1436, although this was less serious than first anticipated. More worrying was the loss of much of Upper Normandy, including the key ports of Harfleur and Dieppe, over the winter of 1435–6, partly as a result of local rebellion. For the first time since the reign of Henry IV, the English were vulnerable in the Channel and had no navy to defend them, as control of Normandy and the Burgundian alliance had prompted a rundown of the navy which Henry V had built up. The loss of Paris in May 1436 was a severe blow to Henry's pretensions to kingship of France, even though the English had already abdicated control of the capital to Burgundy from 1431. The English were able to retain control of many of the towns (such as Pontoise) to the immediate west of Paris but, significantly perhaps, no efforts were ever made to recover the capital. The English had enough to do to recover Upper Normandy and to defend the duchy, 'pays de conquête' and Maine.

Military activities from 1436 were devoted to these ends and to meeting the threat of increasingly frequent French penetrations of the frontiers. Gradually, Upper Normandy was returned to English control although Harfleur was not recovered until November 1441 and, despite sieges in 1442 and 1442, Dieppe remained in French hands. Other major centres on the eastern frontier, such as Evreux and Louviers, fell to the French in 1440–1 and were never recovered. We cannot doubt, however, that the English were determined to hold onto their remaining possessions in the north. There was considerable investment of men and money in the military activities of these years, which suggests that there was still enthusiasm for the war. Whilst much has been made of the difficulties of settling on a suitable royal representative in France once Bedford was dead, there can be no doubt that all of the lieutenants-general chosen were committed to their task of defending the English possessions. Moreover, the English government continued to suppport them as well as it could.[61]

A study of diplomacy, however, reveals the growing realisation that the whole of France could not be secured.[62] At the Congress of Arras in 1435, the English refused to consider the renunciation of the French crown or of any aspect of the Troyes settlement. This was not surprising as they still held Paris and had only recently, as Keen puts it, 'aggressively reasserted' the Treaty of Troyes by having Henry VI crowned as French king.[63] By the time of the next peace negotiations in 1439, however, the English had suffered the loss of Paris and much of Upper Normandy. They were now well aware of the difficult and costly military position, and some divisions of opinion were already emerging in England over war policy. This prompted a willingness at least to consider a temporary dropping of the title in return for the tenure of their holdings in full sovereignty – a virtual return to the 1360 situation, with the addition of the lands they held in northern France. It was realised, however, that the dropping of the title would have considerable implications for the exercise of sovereignty and for those who had been granted lands and privileges by the English kings. In the event, these counter-arguments held sway, although the fact that the English allowed the duke of Orléans to be released after 24 years in captivity implied their continuing hopes for a negotiated settlement.[64]

From 1444 one can detect a considerable shift in the English position. Not only were the English prepared to come to truce (Tours, 28 May 1444) but also they were now thinking of surrendering the claim to the throne in return for little more than Normandy and Gascony in full sovereignty.[65] Two factors seem to lie behind this change of heart. The first was the failure of the expedition of John Beaufort, duke of Somerset, in 1443.[66] This had been intended as a major offensive southwards, perhaps revealing a new commitment to carry the war to the French. It was, however, a campaign planned in England rather than in Normandy, where all military effort was being concentrated on attempts to recover Dieppe. The campaign ended in confusion and in the alienation of Brittany, which Beaufort had chosen to attack. The government was now reluctant to fund another major expedition. By this time too, Gascony was under threat of major French attack for effectively the first time. The second factor was the growing influence in government of Henry VI himself. There is little doubt of his commitment to peace. The Truce of Tours led to his marriage to Charles VII's niece, a clear statement of willingness to settle the dispute. By December 1445 Henry had secretly promised to surrender Maine to the French king, a clear indication that he took neither his French royal title nor the interests of English settlers seriously. Henry thus played into the hands of the French.

Charles took advantage of the truce to reorganise and build up his own army. Whilst his ambitions took shape in the late 1440s, the English could neither settle upon a policy nor afford to maintain a position of military strength from which to negotiate for full sovereignty.[67] This was a traumatic time in English politics in which the problem of France loomed large. The most obvious indication of this was the arrest of the heir to the English throne (and, by virtue of the Troyes settlement, to the French throne too), Humphrey, duke of Gloucester. As Henry V's last surviving brother, his death, probably from a heart attack occasioned by the shock of his arrest, severed an important link with the past, all the more so as he had consistently urged a hard line against Charles VII. Yet even after his removal there remained divisions and confusions over policy which undermined the English war effort. Henry VI's desire for 'peace at any price' was not entirely shared by his ministers or his representatives in France. The dukes of Suffolk and Somerset still had hopes of keeping the French in check: a punitive raid was thus launched in March 1449 on Fougères in Brittany, whose duke was drifting into the French camp.[68] In response, Charles invaded Normandy in August 1449. As a result of financial constraints and confusions in policy on both sides of the Channel, garrisons were too weak to resist, and reinforcements were slow in being dispatched. Local inhabitants offered little support to the English, often betraying their towns to the French.[69] The English suffered an ignominious defeat at Formigny on 15 April 1450, and on 12 August Cherbourg, the last English stronghold, surrendered to the French. The duchy had fallen within a year. Gascony followed suit in very similar circumstances in 1451.

This is, of course, a very bald summary of what happened between 1444 and 1451. But what is most striking is the contrast between Henry VI and Charles VII. Henry offered no strong lead in defence of his French crown or lands, never, for instance, leading an army in person or, in contrast with Richard II, taking a firm line in negotiations. Charles led the invasions of Normandy and Gascony himself, posing as liberator, and with the clear intention of expelling the English once and for all. In such a scenario, English claims to the kingship of France by virtue of the Troyes settlement were scarcely tenable. The treaty had, however, made it very difficult for the English to settle for less. More importantly, it had intended the final displacement of the Valois monarchy and the personal destruction of the Dauphin. Not surprisingly, Charles was never keen on coming to a peaceful accommodation with the English. As in 1420, military success was the eventual arbiter of who should be king of France.

The End of the Hundred Years War

By the middle of 1451 only Calais remained in English hands. The English did not immediately accept this as the end of their continental ambitions. Over the next year serious efforts were made to keep the seas and to reinforce Calais. By the summer of 1452 there were plans to send an army to Normandy, but the promise of aid from Bordeaux led to its diversion to Gascony. As a result, Bordeaux and its surrounding area were recovered. Reinforcements were dispatched in March 1453, and even after

Talbot's defeat and death at the battle of Castillon on 17 July, plans to send more men were not immediately abandoned.[70] With hindsight we can see that Castillon was a major turning point. The English abandoned the reconquest of Gascony and never again held land there or in Normandy, nor did they launch another major assault on France until 1475. That is not to say, of course, that Anglo-French tensions disappeared or that England turned its back on the continent. For the rest of the 1450s Charles VII feared an English attack on Normandy or Gascony and kept large numbers of troops in both areas. Only a lack of cooperation from the duke of Burgundy prevented his launching an attack on Calais, and in 1457 there were serious French raids on southern England.[71] There can be no doubt, however, that these were troubled times in England, partly as a result of the aftermath of defeat in France. This is why the offensive against France was not maintained. The incapacity of the king is the most crucial factor, although it is worth remembering that Henry VI had already shown himself, when *compos mentis*, less than enthusiastic about the war; indeed in a moment of apparent lucidity in 1456 he restated his desire for peace with France.[72] In August 1453 he had succumbed to mental illness, possibly brought on by the news of Castillon. Over the next seven years he was periodically incapable of ruling; a struggle thus developed for control of the government. In its early stages the major contender, Richard, duke of York, saw more advantage in continuing to blame his rival, Edmund Beaufort, duke of Somerset, for the loss of Normandy and Gascony than in advocating a renewal of campaigning.[73]

As the domestic crisis mounted, so foreign policy became 'nothing more than a struggle between factions in England for the friendship of France or Burgundy'.[74] Even before the deposition of Henry in 1461, the Yorkists had courted the Burgundians. After it, the Lancastrians became dependent upon French military aid, eventually driving Edward IV into a formal alliance with Burgundy in 1468. Foreign policy was thus subordinated to domestic concerns. This is also seen in the struggle for control of Calais between York and his opponents in the 1450s. It can be argued that Edward IV only succeeded in taking the crown in 1461 because of support from Calais troops, underpinned by financial aid from the merchants of the Staple at Calais and by an understanding with the duke of Burgundy.[75] In 1470 Henry VI was restored with the aid of Louis XI, but Edward's Burgundian alliance enabled him to seek exile and assistance in Bruges, and to effect his own successful return to England in 1471.[76]

The events of the 1450s and 60s established an important precedent. For the next century or so, the principal influence on English foreign policy was the desire not to recover lost lands but rather to exploit divisions between France and other European powers. In return the French were keen to gain advantage from dynastic upheavals in England; in 1484–5, for instance, Charles VIII was keen to help Henry Tudor in order to prevent Richard III sending aid to Brittany.[77] There seems little doubt that Edward IV's foreign policies were mainly a response to French royal aid for the Lancastrians. This explains his anti-French alliances with Castile, Brittany and Burgundy in 1467–8, and the plans for an invasion of France. (It is interesting to note that the duke of Brittany was prepared to assist him only in the recovery of those lands which the English crown had held in the reign of Edward II, and not therefore for the crown of France or for the Brétigny territories.[78]) Domestic problems pre-empted Edward's invasion plans in the late 60s, but much the same policy was followed once his English crown was secure.[79] From 1472 Edward seems to have been intent upon invading France, perhaps as revenge for Louis XI's role in the events of 1470. In July 1475 he actually did so. There has been considerable debate on both his seriousness and his aims in this campaign. Lander considers that the claim to the throne was a relatively minor element, noting that in the justification for war presented to parliament in 1472, it is only mentioned halfway through and restricted to fourteen lines.[80] The text, preserved in the Letter Book of Christ Church Cathedral Priory, Canterbury, gives much more prominence to the general benefits which war can bring to a nation and to the links with Burgundy and Brittany. Whilst the recovery of Normandy and Gascony is mentioned, a more specific aim may have been the acquisition of the county of

Eu, which Burgundy had offered to deliver to Edward 'if hym lyke to send a puissance to receive it'. A contemporary commentator, Philippe de Commines, considered that Edward never intended to do much in France, but more recently Ross has suggested that Edward was quite serious in his invasion plans until he discovered Burgundy was not prepared to assist him.[81] In the event Edward invaded, but dallied in Calais and soon accepted a pay-off from Louis XI in the form of an annual pension (Treaty of Picquigny, 29 August 1475).

This 1475 campaign has considerable significance. First, whilst English troops were certainly inexperienced because of their long absence from continental warfare and there was limited enthusiasm for war, it was possible to raise an expeditionary army of 11,451 men, larger than any other sent to France in the fifteenth century.[82] Secondly, Louis clearly took the English threat at face value, but more because of the fear of Anglo-Burgundian collaboration than of English claims to territory and crown. Whilst England had been distracted by internal divisions in the 1450s and 60s, Burgundy had replaced her as France's principal enemy. This formed the basis of a new international scene which was perpetuated, after the French defeat of Duke Charles in 1477, by Hapsburg inheritance of the Burgundian Low Countries. Thenceforward Franco-imperial and later Franco-Spanish antagonisms became the principal forces in Europe. On the whole, England's role was secondary: it was merely the ally of France's enemies. Even so, England remained important because of its past relationship with France. Because the French title and claim to lands were never abandoned and full peace never made, the English retained a licence to invade France whenever international circumstances dictated. Even Henry VII, who had no grandiose plans *vis-à-vis* the continent, used the claim to the throne to justify an attack on Boulogne in 1492, although its real aim seems to have been to oppose Charles VIII's annexation of Brittany.[83] As in 1475, the French were anxious to buy off the English. In their turn, Henry's captains advised him to withdraw on the grounds that financially this was his best option and would equal the achievements of English rulers of the past. They made no mention whatsoever of the claim to the throne or to territories in France. The Anglo-French agreement which followed at Etaples was not technically a full peace treaty, but it ensured a cessation of hostilities at least for the lifetimes of the kings who signed it. More importantly, it seems to have been the first occasion since 1422 that a king of France was actually called that by the English in a formal document.[84] The pensions paid to Edward IV and to Henry VII, of between £5000 to £10,000 p.a. were arguably as advantageous to English kings as territorial gain and certainly involved much less hassle and expenditure. Arguably too, French willingness to pay such sums served as tacit confirmation of English rights in France, and of the continuing importance of England in European politics.

A further point needs to be made about the continuing use of the French royal title. It was never made explicit whether Edward IV's claim to it derived from the Treaty of Troyes or from his descent from Edward III. None the less, he was obliged to adopt it in 1461 in order to ensure his secure tenure of the English crown. Henry VI was still alive and could scarcely be left as exclusive holder of the French title, since that would also imply his legitimacy as English king. All subsequent usurpers of the fifteenth century found themselves in the same position. As Shakespeare had his Henry V astutely observe, 'no king of England if not king of France' (Act II, sc. ii). The title thus remained a traditional element in the English royal title. It was also seen as still having a place in the collective memory of the English people – enough to persuade Richard III in 1484 of the value of issuing proclamations which accused Henry Tudor of being prepared to abandon the claim to the French throne and to the former possessions in France in order to win French support for his assault on England.[85]

Recent studies have suggested that Henry VIII may have taken the French claims more seriously, wishing to cut a more prominent figure on the European scene.[86] In the words of David Starkey, he 'had come to the throne determined to renew the Hundred Years War against France'.[87] Certainly the establishment of bridgeheads at Tournai (1513) and Boulogne (1544), although shortlived, marked the first real attempts to conquer territory since 1453. In 1523, a great *chevauchée* across northern France aimed at Paris and possibly even a French coronation; this has recently been termed 'the last campaign of the Hundred Years War'.[88] Henry's policies are difficult to fathom and to generalise. His campaigns are matched by equally showy attempts on several occasions to achieve 'eternal peace' with France.[89] Both Henry's wars and his treaties relate to wider international issues too, now further complicated by religious changes.

After Henry's death policies towards France remained inextricably linked with Spanish and Scottish matters. It was to avenge Mary I's Spanish marriage that the French took Calais in 1558. Yet the sense of France as the ancient enemy was very slow in diminishing, even when Spain emerged as the principal foe. As Lord Burghley remarked in 1589, the year after the Armada, 'the state of the world is marvellously changed when we true Englishmen have cause for our own quietness to wish good success to a French king and a king of Scots'.[90] We must not forget that English armies were active in Normandy in the 1590s, campaigning in defence of the (then Protestant) king of France, Henry IV. The latter appears even to have encouraged the revival of English interests in Calais when faced with an imminent Spanish attack on the town. It is symbolic of the new interests in English foreign policy, however, that to rescue Calais for the French the English chose to attack Cadiz.

As it turned out, therefore, 1453 did mark the end of an era in Anglo-French relations. With the loss of lands in France, the territorial dimension, which had dominated Anglo-French relations since the thirteenth century, evaporated. It is very important that there was a delay of 22 years (i.e. to 1475) before an English army once again entered France. The tenure of Calais offered a small degree of continuity, although it must be remembered that Calais had always been more a military outpost of England than part of 'English France', a status confirmed by its representation in the English parliament from 1536.[91] After 1453, Anglo-French relations were increasingly subsumed within wider European issues. There was no repeat of the intensity of warfare which had persisted before 1453, even under Henry VIII, who spent a quarter of his reign at war with France. With the loss of Calais as an entry point into France in 1558, the value of the claim to the throne as a licence for invasion diminished, although by no means did it end Anglo-French antagonism.

There is danger, however, in drawing too sharp a contrast between a medieval 'Anglo-French War' and an early-modern 'international scene'. The Hundred Years War made England and France inveterate enemies. The loss of territory and English civil war did nothing to change this, and subsequent international politics did much to exacerbate old enmities. Thus none of the peace initiatives of the sixteenth century was able to effect a lasting settlement. Nor can we deny that wider European issues were of vital importance to Edward III and his successors. The Hundred Years War was never waged simply between England and France but it set the two nations on a collision course for several centuries to come.

4

THE WIDER CONTEXT

The European States and the War

The present century has seen two wars deemed worthy of the description 'World War'. The term 'Hundred Years War' emphasises the long duration of Anglo-French conflict rather than its geographical extent. Admittedly, the conflict had little significance outside Western Europe, but within this area it impinged on all countries and formed the main influence on international relations in the later middle ages. Even before the Hundred Years War, Anglo-French relations had loomed large in European affairs. English kings had never been isolationist. Their continental possessions and trading links had always necessitated a close interest in European affairs. Three factors now brought Anglo-French relations to centre stage. The first was the decline of the Empire as the main focus of Europe, a decline already well under way by 1300. The second was the claim of Edward III and his successors to the crown of France. Whether seriously undertaken or not, it elevated the significance of the Anglo-French quarrel within the international context. Thirdly, success in France under Edward III and Henry V made England into a 'superpower', with a formidable military reputation and considerable political influence within Europe as a whole. On the reverse side of the coin, the loss of almost all her French possessions by 1453 reduced England's significance in European affairs, yet it took a while for subsequent English rulers to abandon the notion that the route to greatness in Europe lay through France. For at least two centuries, therefore, English policies towards the rest of Europe, as revealed particularly by the search for allies, were determined by the conflict with France.

Fifty-seven countries were involved in the Second World War. It is not so easy to calculate a figure for the Hundred Years War because it is less obvious what then constituted a country. It is necessary to count non-sovereign territories such as the duchies of Burgundy and Brittany, and the many semi-autonomous units in the Low Countries and Germany, because their rulers were often able to pursue their own policies independent of those of their overlord (in the first two cases the king of France and in the remainder the emperor). Just as technically non-sovereign rulers need to be included, so too do the supranational rulers, the pope and the emperor. A total of about thirty 'countries' can be reached, although they varied much in size and significance.[1] The involvement of other countries was undoubtedly a contributory factor to the difficulty of Anglo-French reconciliation. This was particularly true of Flemish, Breton and Castilian issues in the fourteenth century and of the persistent problem of Scotland. Even when the English and French were technically at peace between 1360 and 1369, their conflict continued through international diplomacy and armed intervention in Castile. Neither of the full peace settlements, at Brétigny and Troyes, solved the international 'sideshows', despite hopes that allies would adhere to their terms. The Treaty of Brétigny, for instance, did not bring an end to the succession dispute in Brittany, although it envisaged that the kings of France and England would act as arbitrators and not renew the war over this issue. The hope that the French would drop their Scottish alliance in return for the English abandoning links with the Flemish was dependent upon controversial and mutual renunciations being performed. The truce of 1396 was intended to embrace allies, but left it to the kings of Castile and Scotland to decide whether they wished to be included.[2] Thus the 'hundred-year' length of the conflict was partly due to the complication of issues outside the principal Anglo-French dispute.

That said, some qualifications need to be noted right at the outset. The first is that the fourteenth-century wars are more worthy of the description 'pan-European' than those of the fifteenth century, as is revealed by the lists of allies included in truces and by the theatres of war. Within the fourteenth century, international involvement was less in the later 1340s and 1350s than it had been in the early years of the war or than it was to be after 1369. Indeed, these contrasts remind us that there were different stages in the conflicts which have been lumped together as the Hundred Years War. Secondly, most of the fighting in the fourteenth century, and almost all in the fifteenth, took place within the frontiers of France. Only a third of our 'countries' saw military action in their own lands as a result of the Anglo-French conflict. Thirdly, it is not possible to divide Western Europe into two distinct camps, one supporting the English and the other the French. Alignments were not always clear cut. In the 1396 truce, both the English and the French claimed the king of the Romans and the Genoese as their allies.[3] Loyalties also changed and many alliances were shortlived, although some, such as the Franco-Scottish, proved long-lasting. Some countries were only involved sporadically in the Hundred Years War, but Scotland was significant throughout. Given its close connections with England and its role in the origins of the war, it is the subject of separate study in the second half of this chapter.

In this respect it is also worth remembering that allies did not always fulfil the obligations of treaties they had entered into. Events soon demonstrated the truth of Pope Benedict XII's warning to Edward III in 1340 of the unreliability of German and Flemish allies.[4] In the early stages of the war, the king of Castile was technically the ally of Philip VI but this did not prevent his attempting to negotiate a marriage alliance with Edward III.[5] Likewise, the terms of the Franco-Castilian alliance of 1406 permitted the Castilians to negotiate annual truces with the English. The situation of Castile is further complicated by the fact that, whilst the king and nobility might be firmly pro-French, her merchants were anxious that their trading interests should not be damaged. This reminds us that the formulation of foreign policy was not as straightforward as we might suppose, or as exclusive to rulers as it was later to become.

There are strong suggestions that the policy towards Spain pursued by the Black Prince from Bordeaux in the 1360s was not the same as that of his father in England. It seems, too, that John of Gaunt allowed his own ambitions to rule his intervention in Spain in the 1380s and in Anglo-French peace negotiations in the early 1390s.[6] An analogous situation arose in the mid-1420s. In pursuing the claims of his wife, Jacqueline of Bavaria, to the counties of Hainault, Holland and Zeeland, Humphrey, duke of Gloucester, waged war against Duke Philip of Burgundy despite the latter's English alliance, and by doing so threw into jeopardy vital support for the double monarchy.[7] In all these scenarios, the danger of English princes with interests in France pursuing their personal line is revealed. If Edward III's policy in France was partly occasioned, as Ormrod has recently suggested, by a desire to create appanages for his sons then doubts can be expressed about the wisdom of his plan, as it threatened to lead to a diffusion of English policies in France.[8] In France the position of the Valois kings was undermined by the ability of the dukes of Burgundy and Brittany and the counts of Flanders to pursue their own foreign policies. The situation in Flanders was further complicated when the major towns conducted negotiations with the English without the sanction, and against the interests, of the count.[9]

Studies of diplomacy during the Hundred Years War have shown just how complicated and convoluted international relations could be.[10] No inhibition was felt, for instance, about conducting simultaneous negotiations with conflicting parties. Indeed, this approach was consciously adopted by rulers in order to gain as much advantage as possible. Allies had to see links with France or England as being in their own interests. Rulers of even relatively minor states were able to retain much independence of action in their dealings with the 'great powers' of England and France, in contrast, perhaps, with the situation in post-medieval centuries. To gain allies English and French kings had to offer considerable sums of money or other benefits. They found it impossible to dictate terms or to ensure definitive loyalty unless allies were totally dependent upon their aid. In this respect, the dependence of Henry of Trastamara on French support for his tenure of the throne of Castile explains his willingness to come to an alliance in 1368 which committed his fleet to attack England and probably also envisaged his invasion of Gascony.[11] Not surprisingly, both the English and the French sought to exploit succession disputes and internal upheavals elsewhere in Western Europe, as the narratives in the previous chapters have demonstrated. Indeed, the fourteenth-century wars are in many ways a series of succession disputes, not only in France but also in Scotland, the Empire, Brittany, Hainault, Flanders and Castile.

This brings us to a fourth qualification. International involvement in the wars was determined by domestic situations in individual countries. English and French foreign policy responded to events elsewhere rather than being the result of long-term planning, and was motivated more by passion than by reason.[12] Unfortunately, it is neither possible nor appropriate to investigate all relevant events in this present work. Nor can we consider other international rivalries and family connections which played their part in influencing alignments during the wars and which the principal protagonists sought to exploit. The Low Countries, for instance, were already the scene of many inter-state disputes over boundaries and vassalage, and thus offered excellent opportunities for both Edward and Philip in the early years of the war, as did the contemporary dispute between the Emperor Lewis of Bavaria and the papacy.[13] Likewise, dealings with Spain need to be seen against a background of continuing Aragonese/Castilian detente. Moreover, the states of Western Europe were not static during the Hundred Years War. Of particular significance for Anglo-French relations was the gradual creation of a Burgundian state within and beyond the frontiers of northern and eastern France. By his marriage to Margaret de Mâle in 1368, Duke Philip the Bold acquired eventual control of Flanders, Artois, Nevers and the county of Burgundy, and by the 1430s, Burgundian rule also extended over Hainault, Holland, Zeeland and Brabant. This created an unprecedented degree of unification in the Low Countries, an area made significant in the early years of Anglo-French conflict by its many separate units. Technically the Burgundian lands were never sovereign and the dukes remained a collateral branch of the Valois line. But in practice ducal powers increased so much that neither their imperial nor their French (nor from 1420 to 1435 their English) royal overlords could exercise much control over them.[14] A further major influence was the papal schism of 1378 to 1417 in which the English and French supported rival claimants. The schism did not owe its origins to the wars, but it was certainly exacerbated by them. In its turn it served as another justification for conflict as well as forcing Western Europe to divide into opposing camps along what were in practice pro-French and anti-French (and hence pro-English) lines.

There are dangers, of course, in seeing the Hundred Years War as a distinct and discrete phenomenon in international relations. English and French kings had already been in conflict before 1337 and had already sought alliances in the hope of advancing their interests and damaging those of the enemy. French links with Castile and Scotland date back to the Anglo-French war of 1294–7, being counterbalanced by Edward I's approaches to Aragon and to the rulers of the Low Countries and Germany. English rulers had sought allies in the last two areas as early as the twelfth century. Much of Edward III's diplomacy at the outset of his wars focused on these very areas, and English interest in them never flagged throughout the Hundred Years War and beyond. The reason was not simply that they were close to or even neighbouring France, although that was clearly an incentive for Edward III in 1337–40, when he needed a continental base from which to attack northern France. An equally significant factor was that they were traditional sources of troops. This partly derived from the semi-independence which many of their rulers enjoyed as a result of the weakness of their imperial overlord. Yet their lack of sovereignty and of resources meant that their support could easily be bought. This is what Edward III did in the late 1330s, much as his grandfather had done in 1297, when he offered financial reward for their military service against France.[15] It is very significant that Edward III followed past precedent in preferring foreign troops for an attack on the French outside Gascony. He was apparently reluctant to raise troops in England, or else foresaw difficulties in trying to do so. Whilst large numbers of men could be raised by foreign alliances (as many as 6000 were promised by May 1337, although only 3000–4000 actually materialised) their service depended on English ability to pay them. As is well evidenced, Edward's financial problems not only delayed the start of his campaigns but also led to the defection of many of his allies in 1341, including the Emperor Lewis of Bavaria, whose support had been bought to enhance Edward's control over his other allies and to justify the first attack into French territory. All of this reminds us of Edward's vulnerability in the early years of the war and of the lack of committed European support for his claim to the French throne. Yet this did not end English interests in the Low Countries and Germany. Whilst no campaigns after 1340 relied on so many foreign troops, alliances involving the provision of men continued to be arranged. Henry V, for instance, sought aid from the Rhineland princes after the Treaty of Troyes as did his son's advisers following the defection of the duke of Burgundy in 1435. Significantly, these fifteenth-century kings also experienced difficulties in paying their allies.[16]

The military significance of alliances merits further consideration. Save at the opening of the war, English reliance on foreign troops was always less than that of the French, and in any case there is little evidence of true mercenary service in either nation's armies. Whilst soldiers of other nationalities can be detected, most come from countries with which the English or French kings had alliances or were on friendly terms. The same conclusion can be reached for maritime assistance. The considerable interest which fourteenth-century English and French kings showed in Castile was largely occasioned by the hope of using the latter's standing navy, or at least of preventing the enemy from doing so. Genoa was also sought as an ally because of its fleet, but as Castile's navy was considerably larger and based in the Bay of Biscay, and as Castile bordered Aquitaine itself, the significance of the Castilian alliance was much greater. The Franco-Castilian alliance of 1368 was a major factor in the decline of English fortunes thenceforward. In response the English sought alliances with Aragon, Portugal and Navarre, and continued to regard Castile as a legitimate theatre of war until

Gaunt abandoned his Spanish interests in 1388. It would be going too far, however, to consider, as one recent French commentator has done, that this period sees the origins of the Anglo-Spanish maritime rivalry which was to loom so large in the age of Elizabeth I.[17] Although the Castilians remained in alliance with the French for the rest of the Hundred Years War, they played little role in its fifteenth-century stages owing to domestic upheavals in both Castile and France, to the decay of the Castilian fleet and to English concentration on northern France. The Flemish, however, remained significant in naval terms. The count's pro-French stance in the 1330s had enabled Flemish ships to be used to lift Edward's attempted blockade of Scotland. The maritime aspect was one element in Edward's desire for a Flemish alliance. Friendly relations with Flanders protected English interests in the Channel and, after 1347, at Calais. This was one reason why a Burgundian alliance was advantageous in the fifteenth century. When relations were cool, as in the early 1400s and after 1435, English insecurity in the Channel increased. The defection of the duke in 1435 also stopped the English transporting their expeditionary armies by the shortest route, from Dover or Sandwich to Calais, for not only were the narrow seas now vulnerable but also the duke's troops controlled the territory of Artois and Picardy which separated the English possessions of Calais and Normandy.

Studies of the relations of England with the Low Countries both before and after Burgundian dominance have demonstrated, however, that trading considerations sometimes mitigated hostile attitudes and led to the mutual desire for truce.[18] The links between trade and the formulation of foreign policy during the Hundred Years War are complex. At first sight, it looks as though royal policies towards trade were subordinated to strategic and political considerations, so that trading links became *victims* as well as *weapons* of war. Anglo-Castilian trade, for instance, was much damaged by Franco-Castilian closeness after 1368.[19] In the late 1330s Edward III put pressure on the rulers of Brabant and Flanders by threats to damage all-important trading links as well as by offers to make substantial trading concessions. Lucas points out, for instance, that the duke of Brabant was won over in 1337 partly by the guarantee of access to English wool, only to vacillate when the promised wool did not arrive.[20] Viewed from another perspective, however, it can be argued that rulers could not afford to damage their country's trading interests for too long. The mercantile lobby in England was strong. Substantial royal revenues and much-needed silver bullion derived from trade.[21] Moreover, Edward III was dependent upon loans from the merchants of the Low Countries for much of the liquid capital in his first campaigns, and subsequently English merchants and towns were important sources of loans for all kings. Thus, whilst trade was used as a weapon of war, it also acted as a restraint on royal policies. It may also have helped to formulate foreign policies in the first place. It is no coincidence that major trading partners were also sought as allies. Indeed, alliances and truces seem often to have been made to preserve and protect trade, one of the best examples being the Anglo-Flemish mercantile truces of the early fifteenth century which were intended to be adhered to even if war broke out between the English and the French.

As England's nearest continental neighbour and premier trading partner, Flanders always played a special role in English policies. At the outset of the war, it had a further significance as the only part of the Low Countries to be a fief of the crown of France. As we have seen in chapter 2, only when Edward could exercise authority in part of France – that is, in Flanders – did he take up the title of king of France. This must be seen against a lengthy background of Franco-Flemish detente, a situation which Edward I had already sought to exploit in his French wars. But circumstances were different in the late 1330s. The count of Flanders was now loyal to the French king: Edward III's alliance was with the count's rebel subjects. This gave Edward some advantages, including the use of Flemish urban militias, but there were fundamental weaknesses in being the ally of rebels rather than of the legitimate ruler. Edward was never able to impose his authority, or even acceptance of his French title, over the entire county. Much the same conclusion can be reached for his subsequent intervention in Brittany. There are dangers, therefore, in portraying Edward III as

entirely successful in exploiting international and local disputes
for his own ends. A more realistic interpretation is that he found
himself embroiled in other people's quarrels, not always to his
advantage. Yet it was by involvement in Flanders and Brittany
that he gained at least some recognition within France of his
claim to be king. In addition, the legacy of poor Franco-Flemish
relations meant that throughout the wars the Valois kings could
never be certain of where the loyalties of the counts and their
subjects would lie, even when the counts were the dukes of
Burgundy and a collateral line of the French royal family.

This brings us back to the significance of the semi-
independent territorial princes within France, for herein lies a
distinctive dimension of the Hundred Years War and one which
was a cause of considerable weakness for the Valois kings when
their title was challenged by Edward III and his successors. As
we shall see, English kings had the constant problem of their
supposed vassal, the king of Scotland. In Aquitaine, too, they
were faced with major vassals who could pursue their own line,
as the events of 1368–9 clearly reveal. But within England their
authority over the nobility was complete. There was no real
parallel of the situation in France, where many nobles were
powerful enough to act against their sovereign and to resist his
centralising ambitions. As Le Patourel observed,

> the first phase of the Hundred Years War, whilst fundamentally a
> war of succession, also showed some of the characteristics of a
> French civil war in which the princes, led by the duke of Aquitaine
> who was also the king of England, fought against the efforts of the
> king of France to make the unity of his kingdom a reality. And they
> were so far successful that the issue between king and princes was in
> doubt for a century or so.[22]

Whilst it can be argued that such resistance to royal authority
pre-dated the war, there can be no doubt that Anglo-French
conflict enhanced and prolonged the independence of the great
feudatories of France. In turn this gave the latter a crucial role to
play in the Anglo-French struggle, all the more so when they
were able to raise large armies, as the Valois dukes of Burgundy
could do.[23] The role of the dukes of Brittany is crucial through-

out the period; Charles and Philip of Navarre played their part in the 1350s. In the fifteenth century, royal weakness and civil war enhanced the significance of all the princes of the blood, most dramatically the Burgundians. Even when the English were finally expelled in 1453 – an act which did much to restore the authority of the French crown – it was to take the Valois another 40 years to effect real control over their great feudatories. Yet it is worth noting that French princes supported English claims only for as long as they saw it in their interests to do so, and that English kings had to offer concessions to them as to their other European allies. Their capacity for independent action could work in favour of the English but it could also work against, as the defections of Philip of Burgundy in 1435 and of Francis of Brittany in 1449 show. English kings could only be realistic claimants to the throne of France if French princes supported them. By the same token, withdrawal of such support was bound to undermine and finally to destroy the English position.

What conclusions, then, can be reached on the international dimension of the Hundred Years War? First, English foreign policies during the conflict were undoubtedly influenced by links forged earlier. But the claim to the French throne gave international dealings a new significance and emphasis since the claim would only be meaningful if recognised by rulers outside, as well as within, France. English kings were not particularly successful in achieving such recognition, but they never ceased to use diplomacy as a means of spreading propaganda for their claim. International acceptance of the Treaty of Troyes was particularly crucial, for it would ensure recognition of the succession of English kings to the French throne and would serve to isolate the Dauphin Charles. Allies were given eight months to decide whether to adhere to the treaty.[24] Responses varied; some accepted its terms, but were reluctant to provide military support without adequate remuneration. The count of Foix's initial adherence ended when Charles offered him the county of Bigorre in 1425. Others, like the prince of Orange, responded by saying they would never acknowledge the rule of 'the ancient and principal enemy of France'.[25] The treaty was never accepted by the Spanish nations, or by the Scots, or, perhaps most significantly, by the papacy. Henry V's failure to win over the whole of Europe thus helped to keep alive hopes of a Valois *revanche*.

Secondly, although there were different stages of conflict and variations in aims, there can be no doubt that English foreign policy from the 1330s onwards was completely dominated by the issue of France. There were already strong moves in this direction from the 1290s. A good illustration of this is provided by royal marriages from the second marriage of Edward I in 1298 to that of Henry VI in 1445. Unless kings and others of royal blood married French princesses in the pursuit of peace, brides were chosen to fortify the anti-French stance. Family relationships played an important role in international dealings, although two reservations must be noted. One is that family connections between Europe's ruling houses were often complicated and contradictory, and did not, therefore, facilitate straightforward alliance systems. The other is that marriages did not in themselves guarantee peace or cooperation; they were seen as a way of bringing sides closer together towards a full settlement, or of cementing existing or recently negotiated alliances.[26]

Thirdly, Anglo-French conflict generated a phenomenal amount of diplomatic business in Europe, encouraging the development of standard international conventions in diplomacy which, once established, persisted into the early-modern period. The roots of this, however, can be seen before 1337. As Cuttino points out, the Treaty of Paris of 1259 generated so many problems that it stimulated Anglo-French diplomacy to an unprecedented degree.[27] A formidable archive of claims and counter-claims continued to be built up, serviced by increasingly specialised lawyers. Diplomacy during the Hundred Years War was still conducted, however, on an *ad hoc* basis; representatives were not maintained on a permanent basis in other countries, nor were there separate departments of state responsible for foreign affairs. Diplomacy was in many respects seen as a legitimate weapon of conflict, an extension of, and a complement to, military activity. The refusal of diplomatic overtures could be exploited as justification to make war, as in Edward III's manifesto of 1337 and Henry V's stance in the summer of 1415.[28] Deliberately staged disputes over safe-conducts, credences and powers, as well as over procedure gave Anglo-French diplomacy a usefully aggressive air. The negotiations at Bruges in 1375, for instance, began with a dispute over precedence in seating arrangements between the dukes of Lancaster and Burgundy. Even the issue of language could be used to tactical advantage: in the discussions of November 1418 the English suddenly raised a spurious objection to the use of French, claiming that they could not understand it.[29] Issues were difficult to settle when the animosity of the battlefield was transferred to the negotiating table. It cannot be denied that diplomacy fostered the growth and, more importantly, the definition of national feeling. In the process each side came almost to see duplicity as a national characteristic of the other. In addition, the very nature of the Anglo-French dispute made it difficult to find common ground for discussion. There was already an impasse over the sovereignty of Aquitaine. The claim to the throne gave both sides even less room for manoeuvre, and international 'side' issues complicated matters further. Truces which aimed at facilitating negotiations were often uneasy and were used rather to provide a breathing space in which to prepare for a renewal of conflict.[30]

There were, however, many attempts to secure peace and to offer mediation. Of particular interest are the interventions of the two 'supranational' rulers, the emperor and the pope. By the early fourteenth century, notions of royal sovereignty were so well developed – indeed, they lay at the root of the Anglo-French conflict – that the kings of the warring kingdoms were scarcely likely to accept papal or imperial dictates or mediation unless it suited them to do so. Emperors might like to see themselves as of importance outside Germany but found it difficult to put this into reality. The title was in practice bandied between the great princes of Germany; repeated succession contests, coupled with lack of royal resources and problems on the eastern frontiers, undermined imperial influence. Whilst the Hundred Years War shows that intractable succession disputes could arise in hereditary systems, the continuing use of the elective principle in the making of emperors generated as much controversy and instability.[31] In brief, emperors were not powerful enough to be impartial in the Anglo-French dispute. They thus sided with whichever protagonist seemed to offer most at any particular time. The papal schism threw them into the English camp, though a desire to end it prompted Sigismund to offer impartial mediation. In the event he came instead to an anti-French treaty with Henry V. Although he was one of the few rulers to recognise the latter's title by the Treaty of Troyes, he failed to provide military aid and the imperial link with England was soon abandoned.

At first sight, the papacy looks an equally unlikely mediator. From 1305 to 1378, almost all popes were French-born; Clement VI had been Philip VI's chancellor before his elevation in 1342.[32] Over this 73-year period, the popes were based at Avignon, close to, although not technically part of, the French kingdom. Not surprisingly, none of them considered Edward III to be king of France. Between 1378 and 1417 there was schism, where the French recognised the pope elected by largely French cardinals at Avignon and the English supported his rival previously elected in Rome. The French popes acknowledged the Valois royal title, the Italian popes the claims of the English kings. Even after the schism was over, Martin V did not accept the Treaty of Troyes, and his successor, Eugenius IV, recognised Charles VII as rightful king of France at the council of Basle in 1434. In addition, papal authority over secular rulers was scarcely as it had been in the early thirteenth century. By the outbreak of the Hundred Years War, kings could already tax their clergy without papal sanction. National churches operated independently and under considerable monarchical influence. This allowed rulers at war, for instance, to request prayers for success against the enemy, and permitted English kings to dispossess French monastic houses of their English lands on the grounds of national security. During the war English kings were frequently in dispute with popes over apparently ecclesiastical issues, most notably the right of papal provision to benefices.[33] Such disputes could well have occurred without the conflict with France, and indeed the Franco-papal relationship was not without its similar discords. But there can be no doubt that the wars exacerbated such issues and complicated papal attempts to mediate as well as encouraging the further development of 'national' churches in France and England.

During the schism, papal mediation was impossible. Indeed, the schism can be portrayed as part of the war. Most obviously it allowed the launching of a campaign in Flanders in 1383, at the expense of the English church, under the guise of a crusade against those who supported the schismatic pope. Yet we must be careful not to dismiss the popes before and after the schism as totally biased in favour of the French and hence of little moment in attempts to reconcile the warring parties. The majority of peace conferences and truces before 1378 were occasioned by papal mediation. Pope Clement VI was involved in person in 1344; papally-appointed cardinals presided over negotiations in 1352–4 and 1375–7, and again at Arras in 1435. Popes did consider that they had a responsibility to ensure peace in Europe. On occasion, their own interests might prejudice peace, but overall it would be true to say that papally-sponsored negotiations and truces failed not because of papal bias but because of the reluctance of the English and French to come to settlement. To submit to papal arbitration was seen as a sign of weakness, and it well suited the English to see the papacy as pro-French. Yet studies of Clement VI and of his predecessor Benedict XII, pope at the outbreak of war, suggest that they were motivated by conservatism rather than by prejudice.[34] For them the dispute stemmed from existing feudal problems. Both found difficulty in taking seriously Edward III's claim to the French throne, for not only did it involve a challenge to a sacramentally legitimate king but also it relied upon those with whom the pope was himself in dispute, Lewis of Bavaria and the Flemish rebels.

Dealings with the papacy, most obviously during the schism, acted as a further complication in an Anglo-French conflict which was already inextricably linked with wider issues of European politics and with many localised disputes. It is easy to come to the conclusion that both the principal quarrel and the 'sideshows' were insoluble save by military ascendancy. Only this could force a settlement, yet it, too, was difficult to achieve given the nature of medieval warfare and the complexity and wide geographical spread of the conflict. Nowhere is this clearer than in the case of Scotland.

Scotland and the Hundred Years War

As we have seen in chapter 2, the issue of Scotland was one of several catalysts leading to the outbreak of Anglo-French war in 1337. Some historians, such as James Campbell, have gone further, suggesting that the immediate cause of this war 'was quite probably the help which Philip VI gave or threatened to give to the Scots'.[35] Like the question of Gascon sovereignty, the Scottish issue was already well established before 1337. More significantly, it had been closely linked to Anglo-French relations for over 40 years, and was to remain so throughout the Hundred Years War and beyond. The issue loomed so large and proved so persistent that Scotland should arguably be treated as one of the theatres in which the Anglo-French conflicts were fought. Scottish involvement in these conflicts had a major impact on relations with England and, as we shall see, did much to ensure Scotland's survival as an independent kingdom.

The Scottish issue, like that of Gascony, revolved around the question of sovereignty. For centuries English kings had claimed to be overlords of their Scottish counterparts but this had meant little in practice and relations had been generally cordial.[36] This peace was irrevocably shattered in the 1290s – a decade which stands not only as the crucial turning point in Anglo-French relations but also in English policies towards Scotland. In both Aquitaine and Scotland Edward I was attempting to clarify and to pursue his rights. In Aquitaine he sought to deny royal sovereignty. In Scotland he sought to promote it. When the principal Scottish royal line came to an end in 1290, Edward was asked to decide between the various claimants. This he used as an opportunity to press his claims to a more active form of overlordship. His intentions were made plain by his collection of chronicle and other materials justifying claims to suzerainty; these parallel similar compilations made to deny French overlordship of Aquitaine.[37] Most Scotsmen did not quarrel with Edward's choice of John Balliol as king. What was more contentious was his insistence on liege homage and on the right to hear appeals from the Scottish royal courts. The parallel with Aquitaine is striking, but, as Barrow notes, there were two crucial differences. First, Aquitaine was not a kingdom, Scotland was. Secondly, English kings had already accepted, albeit grudgingly, the right of the French king to hear appeals; Edward's claim to the hearing of Scottish appeals was a complete innovation and caused immediate problems.[38]

The fundamental rift came when Edward tried to impose another aspect of his overlordship: in June 1294 he summoned Balliol and his magnates to provide military service against France. This war, we must remember, had its origins in Philip IV's attempts to impose his rights over Edward in Aquitaine, and had been made inevitable by the confiscation of the duchy on 24 May 1294. By 23 October 1295 the Scots and the French were in alliance against Edward. The Scots were to invade England if Edward left the country or if he sent large forces against Philip. In return the French king was, if necessary, to give aid to the Scots. In essence, this treaty formed the origins of the 'auld alliance' between France and Scotland which was to threaten England, on and off, until a king of Scotland, James VI, became king of England in 1603. Admittedly, 1295 was not the first time that French and Scottish kings at war with England had sought mutual aid.[39] The 1295 alliance was much more significant than any previous Franco-Scottish link, however, for its very undertaking by the Scots was a clear denial of the type of lordship which Edward I was trying to impose. Not surprisingly, Edward immediately went to war, partly on the grounds that the Scots were rebels against his authority because they were in alliance with his enemies. He demanded that, as a contumacious vassal, Balliol should surrender his kingdom and renounce the French alliance. In the hope of peace, Balliol did both (July 1296), but Edward showed that he was intent upon nothing less than the annexation of Scotland to the English crown. Edward, like his own French overlord Philip IV, saw the value of exploiting feudal custom. But he went further than the letter of the law in attempting to introduce English forms of administration and in denying Scotland's status as a nation.[40]

Subsequent events reflect themes which were to recur in Anglo-Scottish relations for the rest of the middle ages. The first is that the Scots proved themselves quite capable of managing

without a king. Now as later, magnates were able to rally troops
and to offer resistance to the English king. To some degree, the
non-official, quasi-guerrilla response may have proved more
effective than any (inevitably small) Scottish royal army would
have done. Edward's attempted annexation looked at first as
though it might succeed, but the Scots had the added incentive
that they were fighting for their freedom. The wars against
Edward created much stronger Scottish nationalism, particularly
once the magnates had chosen Robert (Bruce) I as king (1306)
and the English had been emphatically defeated at Bannockburn
(1314). In 1320, the Scots made explicit to the rest of Europe by
the Declaration of Arbroath their refusal of English suzerainty
and their belief in their right to independence.[41] As we shall see,
the Hundred Years War was to bring Scotland even more
emphatically onto the European stage and to confirm its status
as an independent nation.

The second point is that Edward I and his successors under-
estimated the difficulty of subduing Scotland by either military
or political means. Yet they refused to abandon their hopes of
doing so. There are strong grounds for thinking that Edward was
forced to come to truce with the French in 1298 in order to
concentrate on Scotland.[42] After Bannockburn, the Scots persis-
tently raided England so that the northern border became
vulnerable and hence costly to defend in a way that it had never
been before. In addition, the Scottish magnates lost their lands in
England by virtue of the breakdown in Anglo-Scottish relations.
This, combined with the strength of Anglo-Scottish hostility,
deprived the English kings of the possibility of using Scottish
troops in their continental campaigns. Thirdly, the removal of
Balliol did not end the Franco-Scottish alliance. It remained in
existence, although then as later, it was the *possibility* of French
aid to the Scots rather than the *provision* of such aid which
caused alarm to the English. Most significantly, the alliance was
confirmed in 1326, at a time when the English and French were
once more at war over Aquitaine: the treaty of Corbeil then
bound Robert I and Charles IV and their heirs to offer mutual
aid against the English in war and peace. Moreover, it explicitly
stated that any future Anglo-Scottish rapprochement would be

nullified by conflict between France and England, for then the Scottish king would be obliged to make war on the English in the name of his French ally.[43]

Anglo-French and Anglo-Scottish relations were thus already inextricably linked before the Hundred Years War began. The 'auld alliance' placed the English king at a great disadvantage, as it tied his hands in his dealings with both the Scots and the French. More worryingly, it raised the possibility of Scottish attacks on northern England during periods of Anglo-French war. As we shall see, English kings were never able to overcome or to overturn this situation. Until 1337, however, the French alliance had played little part in ensuring the survival of Scottish independence: this had been the work of the Scots themselves. To their efforts we can add the weak position of the English after the deposition of Edward II. After another abortive campaign against the Scots in 1327, fought, significantly, in northern England and not in Scotland, the English agreed to a peace settlement in the Treaty of Northampton (May 1328). For the first time, they recognised Robert I as king and drew back from demanding homage. Nor did they demand that Robert withdraw from his French alliance. Effectively, then, the independence of Scotland had been confirmed in 1328, although it must be admitted that this was but a temporary suspension of English ambitions in Scotland. By the mid-1330s Edward III had resumed the offensive. On this occasion, it can be argued that it was specifically the French connection which saved Scotland; the persistence of Anglo-French conflict after 1337 made it impossible for English kings to give their full attention to the subduing of Scotland. Even so, the Scots themselves continued to play an important role in their kingdom's survival.

Edward certainly regarded the Treaty of Northampton as a sell-out. Many of those who supported his seizure of power in October 1330 were of the same opinion; some had the added grievance of having lost lands in Scotland which Edward I had distributed in his moment of triumph. The opportunity to revive fortunes came with the invasion of Scotland by John Balliol's son, Edward, in August 1332. It remains doubtful whether Edward III officially sponsored the latter's attempt to depose the eight-year-old David II who had succeeded Robert I in June 1329. The most we can say is that he did nothing to stop it and that some of his magnates who had lost Scottish lands were certainly implicated.[44] Balliol's success, defeating David's troops at Dupplin Moor on 11 August and being crowned king at Scone on 26 September, came as something of a surprise to all parties. It was clearly now in Edward's interests to support Balliol's cause, all the more so when on 23 November Balliol issued letters at Roxburgh recognising his obligation to pay liege homage to the English king and to provide feudal military service in the British Isles and overseas. These letters imply that Balliol had already made such offers to Edward before the invasion took place.[45] Even better, the Roxburgh letters offered Edward a large area of Scotland to be held in full sovereignty.

These were tempting overtures, offering the prospect of a compliant king in Scotland, who was rendered all the more controllable by his desperate need for English military assistance to secure his rule against that of David II. It is not surprising to find Edward claiming in December 1332 – at the time of the parliament summoned, significantly, to York, a suitable base for action against the Scots – that the Treaty of Northampton was not valid as it was made whilst he was a minor.[46] This argument was also used to explain the lack of persistence in his claim to the French throne in 1328. But it is also interesting to detect in Edward a degree of hesitation and of uncertainty over what he should do about Scotland, characteristics also observable in his behaviour concerning the French crown. Should he proceed towards Scotland and claim direct overlordship as his grand-father had done and take advantage of what was, in fact, a Scottish civil war? Or should he support Balliol and thus base his authority on the Roxburgh letters and on his rights as feudal overlord? Edward's mind was perhaps made up for him by the fact that Balliol was driven out of Scotland in mid-December. To make any gain from the situation it was necessary to provide military support for Balliol. Citing Scottish threats to England as justification, Edward moved his capital to York and, with Balliol in his train, began the invasion of Scotland. This was a major military effort, but it paid off in that David's supporters were defeated at Halidon Hill on 19 July 1333, thus enabling Edward to take Berwick. This was Edward's first great battle, often seen as prefiguring later English victories at Crécy and Poitiers because he used similar tactics of deploying dismounted archers on the flanks. Edward certainly portrayed the battle as the end of the Scottish wars, although in practice the war dragged on with a series of sieges.[47] By June 1334 most of southern Scotland had been transferred to Edward in perpetuity and full sovereignty, and Balliol had paid homage for the rest of his kingdom, but Edward had already drawn back from demanding the right to hear appeals.[48]

How did the French dimension fit into all of this? According to the *Scalacronica*, when Edward and his council discussed Balliol's expulsion in December 1332, they considered themselves free to profit from the situation in Scotland since the Treaty of Northampton had not had any effect upon the Franco-Scottish alliance, and the French were now enemies of the English.[49] The problem is that this was written with hindsight in the 1350s, at a time when French and Scottish affairs had become intertwined and when England and France were openly at war. In 1332–3 Scotland was an issue in its own right. After all, English kings had been at war with the Scots for most of the past 40 years. The advantages of an end to the Franco-Scottish link must have been at the back of Edward's mind, but what he and his magnates sought most of all was to reverse the shameful peace of Northampton and to restore English military pride against the Scots.

At this stage Edward clearly saw Scotland as offering more opportunity than Gascony or than his putative right to the French throne. His willingness to wage war in Scotland further suggests that he did not consider war with the French likely. Thus Edward did not invade Scotland in 1333 to damage the French, although he did try to keep Philip VI ignorant of his plans. Over the next four years, he consistently claimed that what was going on in Scotland was his business alone and that the French king had no right to interfere. Initially Philip showed no inclination to do so, even in the face of approaches from David II's supporters, probably because of his own crusading ambitions. In the spring of 1334, he began to change his tack, perhaps to put pressure on Edward in the discussions concerning Gascony. He may also have been moved by Edward's growing success in Scotland which threatened the loss of any potential advantage a Franco-Scottish link might offer. Whilst his promises of military assistance remained vague, he encouraged David II to take exile in France (May 1334). More significantly, he seems to have insisted to English envoys at this point that David and the Scots should be included in any Anglo-French peace.[50] This proved a major turning point in Anglo-French relations, making a settlement over Aquitaine impossible because of Edward's outrage at Philip's interference in Scotland. According to McKisack, 'Edward was faced with the choice of abandoning his pretensions in Scotland or risking active involvement which might transform a local conflict into a general war'.[51] Her assessment may be going too far, since Philip's interference was scarcely likely to encourage Edward to abandon Scotland completely or permanently. The latter continued to refuse to include the matter of Scotland in his negotiations with the French, but Philip merely responded by briefing his own envoys to restrict their discussions to the very same issue. In August 1335 Edward refused to let Pope Benedict XII act as arbitrator on the grounds that the Scottish issue was a domestic issue, of concern only to the English king.[52] Thus, another impasse was added to that of Gascony, one which contributed to the mounting tension in Anglo-French relations.

Philip's patronage of David II prompted more resistance in Scotland towards Edward and Balliol. By September 1334 their advance had been driven back. Over the next year Edward launched two major offensives, the second consisting of over 13,000 men (an army size only once exceeded in his French campaigns, at the siege of Calais in 1347), but he met with only limited success. The need for constant English military involvement underlined the fact that Balliol was only king by grace of Edward III; this encouraged further resistance. Despite a truce over the winter of 1335–6, there was stalemate and confusion all round. Edward had failed to subdue the Scots, and thus prepared for another offensive in the summer of 1336, whilst also making approaches to David II. Balliol had proved a weak link and seldom left Berwick. Philip had failed to give much aid to the Scots, yet neither had he launched his crusade. A rift with the pope was imminent. On 13 March 1336, Benedict saw fit to postpone the crusade, giving as one reason the continuing problem in Scotland, although it is worth remembering that other issues in Germany and Italy were also cited by him.[53] Now it seems to have been Philip's turn to be outraged, and he may well have diverted his fleet to the Channel in order to launch an attack on southern England in support of the Scots, although no such attack ever materialised. None the less, Edward deemed it best to bring his government back to Westminster in the autumn of 1336. The pressure was thus taken off Scotland. Other issues in Anglo-French relations now began to predominate in the prelude to the confiscation of Gascony. It is interesting to notice, however, that in Edward's manifesto of August 1337, French aid to the Scots was explicitly included as justification for war against Philip VI.[54] This was deliberately aimed at generating support for the war in England, and would surely have struck a nerve in a political and military community which had spent the last three years as equally committed as Edward himself to subduing the Scots.

An independent Scotland had survived the debacle of the late 1330s, but without total dependence on France. As Prestwich observes,

> the Anglo-Scottish problem became, increasingly, a part of the wider struggle of the Hundred Years War, and it became accordingly more difficult to pretend that it was no more than a rebellion against the authority of the English crown.[55]

By 1340 David's supporters had recovered most of the country apart from the extreme south, making Balliol's claim untenable. This success was partly due to the fact that from 1338 Edward's main military and diplomatic focus had been on launching an attack on northern France through the Low Countries. Whilst troops continued to be sent to, and garrisoned in, Scotland in the late 1330s, it soon became clear that the English could not afford to maintain this second front.[56] And a second front it now was.

The connection between the theatres of war is clearly revealed by the ability in 1342 to exchange the earl of Salisbury, taken prisoner in northern France in 1339, for the captured Scottish nobleman, the earl of Moray. The perceived link between the issues is also revealed by suggestions of papal negotiators in 1344 that, for the sake of Anglo-French peace, Edward should abandon Gascony in return for complete control of Scotland.[57] There can be no doubt that Edward's decision to concentrate his military resources on the northern French front made Scotland a more serious threat to English domestic security than it had been at any time since the 1310s. Philip sponsored the return of David II in 1341, partly to encourage military incursions into England.[58] Even without an input of French troops, David raided northern England in 1342 and again in 1345. These raids were now more serious than English penetrations into Scotland. From the French point of view, they helped to counterbalance Edward III's activities in Brittany. David again invaded the north of England in 1346 in the hope of offsetting the disaster of Crécy, a further example of how the war fronts were linked, but was himself defeated and captured at Nevilles Cross (17 October 1346).

Nevilles Cross ought to have given Edward the advantage but, as with the capture of John II at Poitiers, it created new problems. To ransom David would be to acknowledge his kingship. Initially Edward pursued a hard line, demanding a heavy ransom, feudal overlordship, the restoration of lost lands and even the succession of one of Edward's sons to the Scottish throne if David died childless.[59] This was, of course, tantamount to accepting David's right and to abandoning Balliol. Edward is again revealed as an opportunist rather than a man of principle, much as he had been in Brittany too, where he had accepted homage from both the rival claimants. In the 1350s Edward desperately wanted a settlement with Scotland and was even prepared to drop his claim to overlordship and to the succession of his son. We can identify several pressures on him which forced him into an increasingly conciliatory attitude. The first was that the Scots could act independently of their captured king. Edward could not afford the military expenditure to put further pressure on them. Whilst David agreed to most of Edward's initial terms, the Scots were prepared, with French help, to resist having him returned as an English puppet. Secondly, by 1354 Edward may have felt that he had almost come to terms with the French and was anxious that the Scottish issue should not interfere. It is significant that it was at this point that he dropped all his demands save the ransom. Thirdly, the eventual failure of the 1354 peace talks prompted the French to encourage further Scottish incursions into England in late 1355. These were serious enough to prompt Edward to abandon plans for his own campaign in France and to launch a punitive raid into Scotland ('Burnt Candlemas', February 1356). On this occasion he may have toyed with reasserting direct overlordship, as while he was en route Balliol resigned his claim upon the Scottish throne to Edward. But the latter was forced to abandon the campaign after only two weeks when his victualling ships failed to arrive. This, combined with Edward's fears that the unsettled Scottish issue would prevent his taking advantage of the capture of John II at Poitiers, persuaded both sides to agree to the Treaty of Berwick in October 1357. Here Edward accepted a ransom of 100,000 marks for David in order to achieve a truce.[60]

1357 provides an interesting contrast with 1333 in terms of Edward's ambitions in Scotland. To win France, or at least parts of it, he had been compelled over the intervening years to abandon Scotland. Scottish resistance, even in the face of tremendous odds, combined with the continuing implications of the Franco-Scottish alliance, had forced him to return to a situation little different from that of the Treaty of Northampton in 1328. As then, the Scots continued to pose a potential threat, although technically a state of truce prevailed to 1384. David was involved with the French again in 1359 and, when hostilities with France resumed in 1369, Edward considered it politic to lighten the ransom and to extend the truce.[61] Edward was right to think that the Scottish problem would persist. Once it was clear that the English were doing badly, Robert II attacked English-held lands in southern Scotland, although his French links were not strong. The northern border once more became a problem. Once the truce expired there was again a threat of Scottish invasion coordinated with French attacks on the south coast (1385). The English response was to send the feudal host into southern Scotland. Grant sees this as a change from continental to insular ambitions on the part of Richard II.[62] More likely it was a punitive expedition of the sort Edward III launched in 1356 and Henry IV was to lead in 1400. It exemplifies the fact that, with the constraints of their continental interests, English kings could no longer attempt to conquer Scotland. Nor were they in a position to demand homage from the Scottish king or to impose their overlordship, although this claim was never formally abandoned. Edward Balliol was the last king to pay homage, and David II the last king to be asked to pay it, although he never did so.

The Anglo-French wars thus ensured the preservation of effective Scottish independence. Edward III's claim to the throne of France in 1340 and its initial settlement at Brétigny dictated that English interests remain centred on France rather than on Scotland. Ironically, perhaps, the price which Edward III and his successors paid for full sovereignty in an extended Aquitaine in 1360 was the abdication of overlordship of Scotland. There was a further price; this expensive preoccupation with military activity on the continent led to the eventual abdication of control of the frontier with Scotland to magnates who were given large power bases in the north. The northern marches were a militarised zone and thus had a character all of their own. It can be argued that by the fifteenth century these special qualities were conducive to local particularism and potential unrest.[63]

Recurrent conflicts with France in the later fourteenth century kept the Scottish issue alive whilst continuing to hamper the policy of the English kings towards their northern neighbour. The Scottish kings were able to develop their monarchical authority without interference and increasingly without reliance on French aid. Thus it was possible for them to remain nominally a French ally and to continue to pose a military threat to England, as the events of 1388 showed.[64] Interestingly, too, they managed to preserve their independence of action when again without a king, for the future James I had been captured in 1406 when journeying to France. As before, it was Scottish disunity that saved the kingdom, plus the need for the Lancastrian kings to have a peaceful northern border – Henry IV for the sake of the stability of his English crown, Henry V to avoid distraction from his ambitions in France. Peace was thus maintained with Scotland for most of the first half of the fifteenth century, although there were periods of conflict in the late 1410s and 40s, and the border remained in a constant state of defence.[65]

There was less danger of aid to the Scots whilst the French were themselves divided by civil war or threatened by English armies. After Agincourt the French eagerly sought Scottish military assistance. As Anglo-Scottish conflict was now less threatening to Scottish independence, it was feasible for Scottish noblemen to offer their services in France, with the added incentive that such services would be against the old enemy, the English. Of particular significance was the help given to the Dauphin (later Charles VII) from 1419, when the Scottish estates, in the absence of their king, decided to send 6000 men under the son of the Regent.[66] Despite his custody of James I, Henry V failed to prevent Scottish troops serving in France. They played a major role in the defeat of the duke of Clarence at Baugé in March 1421, and received French lands and money in reward. Many met their deaths at Cravant and Verneuil but even this did not end Scottish service in France. The need for Scottish troops was strong enough to prompt Charles VII in 1428 to offer his heir, Louis, in marriage to James I's daughter, along with the territory of Saintonge – offers which testify to the international significance of Scotland as much as to the weakness of Charles. Although James I did not act on this until 1436, Scottish troops crossed on an informal basis in the interim. After his release from captivity in 1424 James maintained the truce with England. By 1436, however, he realised that the English were moving onto the defensive and had lost the Burgundian alliance. He thus felt able to dispatch his daughter and troops to France, and even began to besiege the English-held outpost of Roxburgh in southern Scotland. The English proved less vulnerable than he had thought, and he was forced to abandon the siege. There was soon a further worry for James. As Grant points out, the Anglo-French truce of 1444 was potentially damaging for the Scots, since it meant that the French would no longer need them as allies and, even worse, that the English might be in a position to escalate the border offensive.[67] As it turned out, however, subsequent English disasters in France and civil war at home once more gave the Scots the advantage.

It is worth noting that Anglo-Scottish war continued well after the loss of Gascony in 1453, and that the Franco-Scottish link long persisted as a concern to the English. When Henry VIII invaded France in June 1513, James IV met the terms of his French alliance by invading England, only to meet with disaster at Flodden. In 1544, the French reinforced a Scottish army which raided northern England in response to Henry's attack on Boulogne. With the loss of Calais in 1558 and the future prospect of a Franco-Scottish double monarchy under Mary Queen of Scots and her French husband, it is not surprising to find an English official commenting with some alarm that the French king now bestrode the realm 'with one foot in Calais and the other in Scotland'.[68] Only with the deposition of Mary, the acceptance of Protestantism in Scotland and major changes in the European balance of power was Anglo-Scottish peace established, culminating in the establishment of a double monarchy from 1603.

The matter of Scotland is not restricted to the period of the Hundred Years War. What is clear is that the Anglo-French conflicts of the fourteenth and fifteenth centuries confirmed the survival, and indeed the development, of Scotland as an independent nation. More significantly, Scottish survival was not dependent upon French military assistance. It is a moot point, of course, whether an English king could ever have conquered Scotland, or subdued it to his will. We should have no doubt that Edward III enjoyed more success in France than in Scotland. To understand the reasons for this, one should not spend too long, I think, comparing the validity of his claims to lands and titles in both areas. One should perhaps drive from London to Edinburgh to realise just how far away Scotland is compared to Calais and Normandy, and how relatively inaccessible at a time when sea transport had advantages over land travel. Even the conquest of southern Scotland had proved difficult, let alone any further penetration into the highland areas. The second thing one should do is to read the account by Froissart of the 1327 campaign in Weardale.[69] The descriptions of Scottish military organisation and provisioning therein provide clues as to why the English found it easier to defeat the French than the Scots. Whilst there is much truth in the observation that the Hundred Years War saved Scotland, it can be argued that Edward III had already shown himself to be unable to subdue the Scots even before he began to tackle the French. Moreover, by the mid-fifteenth century, the English had lost not only their hundred-year-war against France but also their hundred-and-fifty-year war against Scotland.

CONCLUSION

My five-year-old son keeps asking me who won the Hundred Years War. To him the question seems both sensible and valid, for all wars surely have winners and losers. When time is short I usually tell him that the French won. After all, they did overcome English armies at Formigny in 1450 and Castillon in 1453, defeats which the English were never able to redeem. As a result Normandy and Gascony were lost. Never again were the English to hold lands on such a scale in France; the tenure of Calais in 1558 and briefly-held Tudor conquests provided but a pale reflection of former glories. Victory in the early 1450s was both a symptom and a cause of the strengthening of the French monarchy thenceforward. The development of absolutism was only made possible by mastery of the whole of geographical France. The expulsion of the English from Normandy and Gascony was a necessary first step; by the end of the century, Brittany and most of Burgundy had also been absorbed. By contrast, the aftermath of 1450–3 for England was political upheaval and civil war. Both Yorkist and Tudor usurpers had to devote much attention to the rebuilding of royal authority at home – so much, perhaps, that foreign ambitions had to be given second place. Yet once royal authority was re-established, England again became a formidable force in the European scene, whether as ally or as enemy to the French.

International relations were as fluid in the middle ages as in later centuries. In this context the use of the term 'Hundred

Years War' proves a considerable disadvantage, for it makes it look as though there was one continuous war which the French finally won. My little boy is often rather confused by the notion of a French victory. After all, the only other thing he knows about the Hundred Years War is that the English emphatically defeated the French at three major battles. If, however, I have enough time to explain to him that there were different stages of the Hundred Years War, the significance of these victories is more easily absorbed. The simple notion of a final French victory overlooks the fact that in 1360 and in 1420 the English had, to all intents and purposes, won their wars. It is true that none of the three great battle successes led directly to French acknowledgement of English victory. But they played a considerable part in making possible the settlements of 1360 and 1420, both of which were dictated by English desires. We must assume that Edward III and Henry V respectively considered these settlements as giving them what they wanted.

Yet they are very different settlements. Brétigny (1360) was essentially a settlement to a feudal conflict. In effect it was the logical resolution of growing English annoyance over the terms of the Treaty of Paris of 1259. Edward III used his victories to gain the full sovereignty over Gascony which Edward I and Edward II had argued was rightly theirs. In the process he expanded the extent of English dominions in France. That he was able to achieve both sovereignty and an increase in territory was due largely to his military achievements. But success in war was arguably facilitated by the claim to the throne. The claim entitled him to wage war against France on a scale which his predecessors could not have done.

In the middle ages wars had to be fought for just causes. English kings to 1337–40 were constrained by the Treaty of Paris and by the acts of homage which had subsequently been paid. Together these gave the advantage in terms of 'just cause' to the French king. The feudal relationship worked in his interests rather than those of his vassal – all the more so when the intrinsic *feudal* authority of the French king was enhanced by the increase in his *royal* power over the course of the thirteenth century. Edward III's claim to the throne made the conflict one between equals rather than between lord and vassal. Given the level of military success he achieved in France, he was able to use the claim to advantage as a bargaining counter in the peace negotiations of the late 1350s. By transforming the war into a dynastic struggle, Edward was able to effect a settlement to the feudal issue. We can see this with hindsight, but we can only assume that contemporaries saw it likewise. We will never know precisely why Edward claimed the throne or whether he seriously entertained the possibility of becoming king of France. All we can be sure of is that in 1360 he was willing to give up the title and probably the claim too. But he only did this in return for complete victory in the old feudal conflict. The settlement was intended to end the feudal authority of the French king and in practice was also a dismemberment of the French kingdom.

Between 1360 and 1420 English interests focused on the maintenance of this settlement. The English war aim after 1369 was, initially, to defend and, subsequently, to restore the Brétigny/Calais terms. This seems to be true even of the campaigns of Henry V, at least up to the end of 1419. The basic problem was that Charles V had refused to adhere to the 1360 settlement. The only means he had at his disposal to challenge the settlement was to revive the old notions of French feudal supremacy. The only weapon the English had was a renewal of the claim to the throne. But it seems highly unlikely that this claim was seen by the English as more than a bargaining counter in this phase of the war. After all the English position was irrevocably weakened by the fact that Edward III had given up the title in 1360. Moreover, the wars from 1369 to 1419 were indecisive, so that the French could not be forced to return to the Brétigny terms nor could the English be persuaded to drop them.

Only when the French position seriously deteriorated in the late 1410s were they forced into a settlement. Henry V's military success forms part of the explanation for this but it was not enough by itself; severe internal dislocation in France was also needed. The gravity of the situation is revealed by the kind of settlement which Troyes (1420) was. In order to win the civil war and to exclude the 'duke-slaying' Dauphin from the throne the Burgundians were prepared to accept Henry as heir to the French throne. The years 1419–20 saw a dynastic crisis in France far more serious than that of 1316 or 1328. It caused a fundamental change in the position the English had held since 1369 – the desire to restore the Brétigny settlement – with the addition of an ambition for a similarly fully sovereign Normandy under Henry V. It could be said, therefore, that the Treaty of Troyes was a dynastic settlement to a feudal war. A 'legitimate' French king nominated the king of England as his heir, and two years later, a king of England was recognised as king of France by some Frenchmen. Thenceforward the war was for the crown of France, for just as the English had found it impossible to give up their belief in the Brétigny settlement so too they could not renege on Troyes.

A further observation is that the wars were won and lost in France. Whilst the level of English input is clearly significant (no more so than in the late 1440s) it was the response of the French which mattered. Henry V's military success was arguably no greater than that of Edward III but political circumstances in France gave him a speedier, and at first sight a greater, victory. But an English ruler as king was never really acceptable to the French. Edward III had not been able to impose much of his supposed French kingship on France. Henry VI was slightly more successful but only for as long as the French royal family and nobility were divided. Here perhaps we can conclude that save for the unusual circumstances of 1419 to 1435, the French nobility might be prepared to tolerate an English king as a fellow peer of France or even as an independent ruler of part of it, but not as their king. The rest of the population might be prepared to accept whoever was able to impose authority over them, but were thus only loyal to the English for as long as the latter's military and political control was effective. Moreover, once Henry VI had failed in his exercise of royal power, it was impossible for him to return to being a feudal vassal or even a sovereign ruler of part of France. Neither English nor French pride could allow it. Troyes was an all or nothing settlement. By 1558 the English had nothing save an empty title. But as Troyes had made an English king king of France, the title itself was no longer negotiable. Truces could be arrived at, but the title could not be surrendered until France had rid itself of a monarchy altogether.

In conclusion we might suggest that the Brétigny settlement was just about workable, both for the English and for the French: the Troyes settlement was not. Even if Henry V had lived longer it is difficult to believe that his kingship of the whole of France would have been recognised or secured. Both settlements were the result of the specific circumstances which produced them. They became untenable when circumstances changed, and the most significant factor in this was the accession of a new ruler. Indeed all changes of rulers, whether in France, in England, or in neighbouring royal or non-royal dynasties, were very significant to Anglo-French relations. In this respect the notion of a Hundred Years War is misleading. Up to the coining of the term the approach of historians had been reign-based, and in many ways this has much to merit it.

Another suggestion also presents itself. Normally we see the peace settlements as the ends of wars but it might also be wise to cite them more obviously as the origins and causes of conflict in their own right. In this scenario the wars of Edward III up to 1360 were still the 'wars of the Treaty of Paris (1259)', as those of his father and grandfather had been; the claim to the throne added a new dimension and as noted above gave Edward an advantage which his predecessors had not enjoyed. The wars from 1369 to 1420 were the 'wars of the Treaty of Brétigny'; and those from 1420 to 1453 the 'wars of the Treaty of Troyes'. There can be no doubt that all of these wars rank high as amongst the most serious conflicts in medieval Europe and that in their time they formed the crux of the international scene. It is highly unlikely, however, that England and France would have enjoyed peace even if Edward III had not claimed the throne. They remained enemies long after the claim was meaningless and English lands in France were lost. The legacy of what the British Agriculture Minister recently called a 'thousand years of rivalry and hatred' is still being played out, but with trawler nets and fisheries protection vessels rather than with cavalry and longbows.[1]

NOTES

Abbreviations Used in the Notes

BIHR	*Bulletin of the Institute of Historical Research*
EcHR	*Economic History Review*
EHR	*English Historical Review*
Foedera	Thomas Rymer, *Foedera, conventiones, litterae et cujuscunque generis acta publica* (third edition, The Hague, 1739–45, unless otherwise stated)
P+P	*Past and Present*
Rot. Parl.	*Rotuli Parliamentorum*, ed. J. Strachey *et al.* (London, 1767–7)
TRHS	*Transactions of the Royal Historical Society*

INTRODUCTION

1. For eleventh- and twelfth-century interests see J. Le Patourel, *The Norman Empire* (Oxford: Clarendon Press, 1976) and for the period from 1154 to 1259 J. Gillingham, *The Angevin Empire* (London: Arnold, 1984).
2. J. Sumption, *The Hundred Years War* (London: Faber, 1990).
3. C. T. Allmand, *The Hundred Years War c.1300–c.1450* (Cambridge University Press, 1988) offers a comparative study of English and French experiences and provides a comprehensive bibliography. E. Perroy, *The Hundred Years War* (first pub. in French 1945, Engl. trans. New York: Capricorn Books, 1965) remains the best one-volume narrative of the whole war.

1 THE HUNDRED YEARS WAR AND HISTORIANS

1. K. A. Fowler, *The Age of Plantagenet and Valois* (London: Elek Press, 1967), pp. 13–14, although Fowler is more convinced than I am that contemporaries had some notion of a 'hundred year' war.

2. F. Taylor and J. S. Roskell (eds), *Gesta Henrici Quinti. The Deeds of Henry the Fifth* (Oxford: Clarendon Press, 1975), introduction, parts II and III.

3. We are fortunate for the English side in having two very helpful recent surveys: A. Gransden, *Historical Writing in England, II: c. 1307 to the early sixteenth century* (London: Weidenfield, 1982) and J. Taylor, *English Historical Literature in the Fourteenth Century* (Oxford: Clarendon Press, 1987). There is also C. L. Kingsford's older but still valuable *English Historical Literature in the Fifteenth Century* (Oxford: Clarendon Press, 1913). Subsequent comments on chroniclers are derived, unless otherwise stated, from these works. Gransden includes some discussion of writers based in France, but for French chronicles in general see A. M. L. E. Molinier, *Les Sources de l'histoire de France des origines aux Guerres d'Italie, 1494*, vol. IV (Paris: Picard, 1901). A Europe-wide list of published chronicles is provided by J. M. Bak, *Medieval Narrative Sources: A Chronological Guide* (New York and London: Garland, 1987).

4. F. W. D. Brie (ed.), *The Brut*, vol. II (Early English Text Society, old series 136, 1908), pp. 572–84. C. T. Allmand, *Lancastrian Normandy, 1415–50* (Oxford: Clarendon Press, 1983), pp. 253–4.

5. *Adae Murimuth Continuatio Chronicarum*, ed. E. M. Thompson (London: Rolls Series, 1889), pp. 200–4, 212–17; A. E. Prince, 'A letter describing the battle of Nájera in 1367', *EHR*, 44 (1926), 417. See also K. A. Fowler, 'News from the Front: Letters and Despatches of the Fourteenth Century', in *Guerre et Société en France, en Angleterre et en Bourgogne XIVe–XVe siècle*, ed. P. Contamine, C. Giry-Deloison and M. H. Keen (Lille: Université de Charles de Gaulle, 1991), pp. 63–92.

6. *The Great Chronicle of London*, ed. A. H. Thomas and I. D. Thornley (London: Jones, 1938, reprinted by Alan Sutton, 1983), pp. 109–21; *Chronique du Religieux de Saint Denis*, ed. M. L. Bellaguet (Paris, 1852), XVI, pp. 410–31; *Chronique d'Enguerran de Monstrelet*, ed. L. Douet d'Arcq (Paris: Société de l'Histoire de France, 1859–62), III, pp. 390–402; *Recueil des croniques et*

anchiennes istories de la Grant Bretagne a present nomme Engleterre par Jehan de Waurin, ed. W. and E. L. C. P. Hardy (London: Rolls Series, 1868–84), II, pp. 304–16; *Chronique de Jean le Fèvre*, ed. F. Morand (Paris: Société de l'Histoire de France, 1876–81), II, pp. 3–8.

7. Molinier, *Sources*, p. 1. See also G. M. Spiegel, *The Chronicle Tradition of Saint-Denis. A Survey* (Brooklyn and Leyden: Classical Folio Editions, 1978), pp. 121, 129.

8. Gransden, *Historical Writing*, p. 60, although I have been more exact on the terminations of Baker and Avesbury, both of whom Gransden says close with the battle of Poitiers.

9. *Murimuth*, pp. 100–1.

10. *Robertus de Avesbury De Gestis Mirabilibus Regis Edwardi Tertii*, ed. E. M. Thompson (London: Rolls Series, 1889), p. 279.

11. Most recently J. J. N. Palmer, *Froissart: Historian* (Woodbridge: Boydell and Brewer, 1981) and P. F. Ainsworth, *Jean Froissart and the Fabric of History. Truth, Myth and Fiction in the Chroniques* (Oxford: Clarendon Press, 1990).

12. Froissart, *Chronicles*, ed. G. Brereton (London: Penguin, 1968), p. 37.

13. Taylor, *English Historical Literature*, p. 158.

14. M. H. Keen, 'Chivalry, heralds and history', in *The Writing of History in the Middle Ages*, ed. R. H. C. Davis and J.M. Wallace-Hadrill (Oxford: Clarendon Press, 1981), p. 410; *Monstrelet*, I, p. 4.

15. *Chronique de Jean Le Bel*, ed. J. Viard and E. Déprez (Paris: Société de l'Histoire de France, 1904), I, pp. 1–2, II, pp. 65–7.

16. *Monstrelet*, I, pp. 2, 5; *Waurin*, I, p. 2.

17. *Monstrelet*, I, p. v.

18. Ainsworth, *Jean Froissart*, p. 7.

19. The Chandos herald's work is translated in R. Barber (ed.), *The Life and Campaigns of the Black Prince* (Woodbridge: Boydell and Brewer, 1979).

20. London, College of Arms, Ms 9. See B. J. H. Rowe, 'A Contemporary Account of the Hundred Years War from 1415 to 1429', *EHR*, 41 (1926), pp. 504–13.

21. *Monstrelet*, I, p. 2; *Le Bel*, I, pp. 155–6, and also his contrast of Edward III and Philip VI, II, pp. 65–7.

22. J. Speed, *The History of Great Britain under the Conquests of the Romans, Saxons, Danes and Normans* (London, 1611), p. 573.

23. H. E. Hallam, *View of the State of Europe During the Middle Ages*,

first edition 1818, cited from ninth edition (London: Murray, 1846), I, p. 48

24. Sumption, *Hundred Years War*, p. x.

25. H. Ellis (ed.), *Three Books of Polydore Vergil's English History* (London: Camden Society, first series, 1844), p. xxviii.

26. Ibid., pp. 82–3, 77 and 93 respectively.

27. Palmer, *Froissart: Historian*, pp. 2–4; *Monstrelet*, I, p. x.

28. E. Hall, *The Union of the Two Noble and Illustrious Families of Lancaster and York*, ed. H. Ellis (London 1809, reprinted New York: AMS Press, 1965).

29. G. Bullough, *Narrative and Dramatic Sources of Shakespeare* (London: RKP, 1960), 3: *Henry VI*, esp. pp. 24–5. For *Henry V* see vol. 4 (1962).

30. W. S. Churchill, *A History of the English-Speaking Peoples*, vol. 1 (London: Cassell, 1956), p. 317. The duke's comment is cited in A. R. Myers, 'The Character of Richard III' in *English Society and Government in the Fifteenth Century*, ed. C. M. D. Crowder (London: Oliver and Boyd, 1967), p. 112.

31. C. L. Kingsford (ed.), *The First English Life of Henry the Fifth* (Oxford: Clarendon Press, 1911), p. 4.

32. Berners' preface as cited in R. M. Smith, *Froissart and the English Chronicle Play* (New York: Columbia University Press, 1915), p. 32; S. J. Gunn, 'The French Wars of Henry VIII', in *The Origins of War in Early Modern Europe*, ed. J. Black (Edinburgh: Donald, 1987), pp. 28–51.

33. P. Morgan, *War and Society in Medieval Cheshire 1277–1403* (Manchester: Cheetham Society, third series, 34, 1987), pp. 3–5; J. G. Nichols (ed.), *The Chronicle of Calais* (London: Camden Society, first series, 1846), noting particularly the list of participants in the 1492 campaign on pp. 2–3.

34. See for instance the *Catalogue of the Library, Overstone Park* (privately printed, 1867). The principal part of the collection was formed from the 1820s by J. R. McCulloch, added to from the 1860s by Samuel Jones Lloyd, Baron Overstone, and bequeathed to the University of Reading in 1920. I am grateful to David Knott of the University Library for his help in locating and consulting early editions of chronicles and historical works.

35. M. McKisack, *Medieval History in the Tudor Age* (Oxford: Clarendon Press, 1971), esp. chapters 3 and 4; R. B. Wernham, 'The Public Records in the Sixteenth and Seventeenth Centuries', in *English Historical Scholarship in the Sixteenth and Seventeenth Centuries*, ed. L. Fox (Oxford: Clarendon Press, 1956), pp. 11–30.

E. Hallam, 'Nine Centuries of Keeping the Public Records', in *The Records of the Nation. The Public Record Office 1838–1988: The British Record Society 1888–1988*, ed. G. Martin and P. Spufford (Woodbridge: Boydell and Brewer, 1990), pp. 23–40.

36. M. Nortier, 'Le sort des archives dispersés de la Chambre des Comptes', *Bibliothèque de L'Ecole des Chartes*, 123 (1965), pp. 460–537; C. T. Allmand, 'The Collection of Dom Lenoir', *Archives*, 6 (1964), pp. 202–10. For an example of an early guide to governmental records see J. Strachey, *An Index to the Records with Directions to the Several Places where they are to be found* (London, 1739).

37. T. Carte, *General History of England* (London, 1750), II, pp. iii, 429.

38. M. McKisack, 'Edward III and the Historians', *History*, 45 (1960), p. 2.

39. D. Hume, *History of England from the Invasion of Julius Caesar to the Rebellion in 1688* (first pub. 1770; revised edn London, 1823–4), I, p. 392; R. Henry, *History of Great Britain* (first pub. Edinburgh, 1771–85; third edition, 1800), p. 205; R. de Thoyras, *History of England* (London, 1732), I, p. 530.

40. Cited in Palmer, *Froissart: Historian*, p. 4.

41. For Balzac's comment, see G. Duby, *The Legend of Bouvines* (English edition, Cambridge University Press, 1990), p. 136.

42. McKisack, 'Edward III', pp. 3–4.

43. C. T. Allmand, *Henry V* (London: Historical Association G68, 1968), pp. 6–8.

44. G. P. Cuttino, 'Historical Revision: the Causes of the Hundred Years War', *Speculum*, 31 (1956), pp. 463–77.

45. M. G. A. Vale, 'England, France and the Origins of the Hundred Years War', in *England and her Neighbours 1066–1453. Essays in Honour of Pierre Chaplais*, ed. M. C. E. Jones and M. G. A. Vale (London: Hambledon Press, 1989), pp. 199–216. For full bibliographical details of the views cited in this section see this article and that of Cuttino cited in the previous note.

46. G. Templeman, 'Edward III and the Beginnings of the Hundred Years War', *TRHS*, fifth series, 2 (1952), pp. 69–88.

47. M. G. A. Vale, *The Angevin Legacy 1250–1340* (Oxford: Blackwell, 1990) and his previous works cited therein.

48. P. Lewis, 'France and England', in *Britain and Europe. Ten Centuries*, ed. D. Johnson, F. Crouzet and F. Bedarida (Folkestone: Dawson, 1980), p. 32. Churchill also saw the wars as 'a continuation of the long revenge of history for the Norman

Conquest of England', *History of the English-Speaking Peoples*, 1, p. 316.
49. See Select Bibliography for details of most of these works. Allmand, *Hundred Years War* contains the fullest and most recent bibliography.
50. J. Le Patourel, 'Edward III and the kingdom of France', *History*, 43 (1958), pp. 173–89; J. J. N. Palmer, 'The War Aims of the Protagonists' in *The Hundred Years War*, ed. K. A. Fowler (London: Macmillan, 1971), pp. 69–70.
51. G. Bois, *The Crisis of Feudalism* (first pub. in France 1976, Engl. trans. Cambridge University Press, 1984), p. 335. On the debate on costs to England see particularly M. M. Postan, 'Some social consequences of the Hundred Years War', *EcHR*, 12 (1942), 1–12; K. B. McFarlane, 'War, the economy and social change. England and the Hundred Years War', *P+P*, 22 (1962), 3–13; M. M. Postan, 'The Costs of the Hundred Years War', *P+P*, 27 (1964), 34–53; A. R. Bridbury, 'The Hundred Years War: Costs and Profits', in *Trade, Government and Economy in Pre-Industrial England. Essays presented to F. J. Fisher*, ed. D. C. Coleman and A. H. John (London, 1976), pp. 80–95.
52. Allmand, *Hundred Years War*, p. 3.
53. D. Goulay, 'La Résistance à l'occupant anglais en Haute-Normandie, II', *Annales de Normandie*, 36 (1986), 92–6.
54. K. B. McFarlane, *The Nobility of Later Medieval England* (Oxford: Clarendon Press, 1973), p. 5, although he suggests that the war was fought from the time of Edward I to that of Henry VIII.

2 ORIGINS AND OBJECTIVES: ANGLO-FRENCH CONFLICT IN THE
FOURTEENTH CENTURY

1. C. W. Hollister, 'Normandy, France and the Anglo-Norman regnum', *Speculum*, 51 (1976), 202–40 provides a useful discussion of Norman and Angevin attitudes to the payment of homage.
2. *Foedera*, I, p. 37; W. L. Warren, *King John* (first pub. 1961, London: Penguin, 1966), pp. 70–2.
3. This is not the first known appeal. For an example of 1171 see P. Chaplais, 'English arguments concerning the feudal status of Aquitaine in the fourteenth century', *BIHR*, 21 (1946–8), 203.
4. *Foedera*, I, pp. 177–8.
5. M. G. A. Vale, 'The Gascon Nobility and Crises of Loyalty 1294–1337', in *La 'France Anglaise' au Moyen Age. Actes du IIIe*

Congrès des Sociétés Savantes, Poitiers 1986 (Paris: CTHS, 1988), pp. 207–16, and his *Angevin Legacy*, chapter 4.

6. M. Wade-Labarge, *Gascony. England's First Colony 1204–1453* (London: Hamish Hamilton, 1980), pp. xii, 13, 54–61 and passim for what follows; P. Chaplais, 'The Chancery of Guyenne 1289–1453', in *Studies Presented to Sir Hilary Jenkinson*, ed. J. C. Davies (Oxford: Clarendon Press, 1957), p. 64, reprinted in P. Chaplais, *Essays in Medieval Diplomacy and Administration* (London: Hambledon Press, 1981); Vale, *Angevin Legacy*, pp. 141–2.

7. For the text of the treaty see *Foedera*, I, ii, p. 45, and *English Historical Documents*, vol. III, ed. H. Rothwell (London: Eyre & Spottiswoode, 1975), pp. 376–9.

8. R. Studd, 'The "Privilegati" and the Treaty of Paris', in *La France Anglaise*, pp. 175–9.

9. Vale, *Angevin Legacy*, pp. 49–50; Wade-Labarge, *English Gascony*, pp. 37–8.

10. The relevant set of documents is in *Foedera*, I, ii, pp. 179–80; H. Johnstone, 'The County of Ponthieu, 1279–1307', *EHR*, 29 (1914), 436–7.

11. J. Glenisson, 'L'application de la "paix" de Paris en Saintonge de 1273 à 1293' in *La France Anglaise*, pp. 201–4.

12. Vale, *Angevin Legacy*, pp. 63–79; E. H. Shealy, 'The persistence of particularism; the county of Ponthieu in the thirteenth and fourteenth centuries', in *Documenting the Past. Essays presented to G. P. Cuttino*, ed. J. S. Hamilton and P. J. Bradley (Woodbridge: Boydell, 1989), pp. 34–6, 39–40.

13. Vale, *Angevin Legacy*, pp. 179, 187–9.

14. Ibid., p. 176.

15. Chaplais, 'English Arguments', pp. 205–11.

16. *Foedera*, I, iv, pp. 24–9.

17. P. Chaplais, 'Le Duché-pairie de Guyenne: l'hommage et les services féodaux de 1303 à 1337', *Annales du Midi* (1958), 147–8, reprinted in his *Essays in Medieval Diplomacy*.

18. See for instance *The Gascon Calendar of 1322*, ed. G. P. Cuttino (London: Camden Society third series 70, 1949).

19. *Foedera*, II, ii, pp. 136–8, and 141–2 for the grants to Prince Edward of Ponthieu and Aquitaine.

20. M. Jusselin, 'Comment la France se préparait à la Guerre de Cent Ans', *Bibliothèque de L'Ecole des Chartes*, 73 (1912), 211, 220–2.

21. *Foedera*, II, ii, pp. 185, 187.

22. Ex info. P. Contamine. The best discussion in English remains

J. Potter, 'The development and significance of the Salic Law of the French', *EHR*, 52 (1937), 235–53.

23. *Foedera*, II, ii, 743 (Record Commission Edition, 1816–69). This document is not included in the Hague edition).

24. P. Chaplais, 'Un message de Jean de Fiennes à Edouard II et le projet de démembrement du royaume de France (janvier 1317)', *Revue du Nord*, 43 (1961), 145–8, reprinted in his *Essays in Medieval Diplomacy*.

25. *Foedera*, II, ii, p. 185; Vale, *Angevin Legacy*, pp. 196–8, 229–30, 237–8.

26. H. Stein, 'Les Conséquences de la bataille de Cassel pour la ville de Bruges et la mort de Guillaume de Deken, son ancien bourg-mestre (1328)', *Bulletin de la Commission Royal d'Histoire*, 68 (1899), 656. See also H. Pirenne, 'La Première tentative faite pour reconnaître Edouard III d'Angleterre comme roi de France (1328)', *Annales de la Société d'Histoire et d'Archaeologie de Gand*, 5 (1902), 5–11.

27. H. S. Lucas, *The Low Countries and the Hundred Years War 1326–47* (University of Michigan, 1929, reprinted Philadelphia: Porcu-pine Press, 1976), p. 80.

28. Ibid., p. 83.

29. *Foedera*, II, ii, p. 740 (Record edition); R. Nicholson, *Edward III and the Scots* (Oxford: Clarendon Press, 1965), pp. 48–9.

30. Ibid., p. 51.

31. Lucas, *Low Countries*, p. 80; E. Déprez, *Les Préliminaires de la Guerre de Cent Ans* (Paris, 1902, Geneva: Slatkine-Megariotis Reprints, 1975), p. 39, n.3.

32. R. Cazelles, *La Société politique et la crise de la royauté sous Philippe de Valois* (Paris: Librarie d'Argences, 1958); N. B. Fryde, *The Tyranny and Fall of Edward II* (Cambridge University Press, 1979).

33. Déprez, *Préliminaires*, p. 39.

34. Ibid., p. 40; Jusselin, 'Comment la France', pp. 222–6.

35. *Foedera*, II, iii, p. 27; *Murimuth*, pp. 58–9.

36. Vale, *Angevin Legacy*, pp. 249–50.

37. *Rot. Parl.*, II, p. 67; Nicholson, *Edward III and the Scots*, p. 100; E. Déprez, 'La Conférence d'Avignon 1344: l'arbitrage pontificale entre la France et l'Angleterre', in *Essays in Medieval History presented to T. F. Tout*, ed. A. G. Little and F. M. Powicke (Manchester University Press, 1925), p. 314.

38. *Les Grandes Chroniques de France*, vol. IX, ed. J. Viard (Paris: Société de l'Histoire de France, 1937), pp. 152–3.

39. *Foedera*, II, ii, p. 187, translated in *English Historical Documents*, vol. IV, ed. A. R. Myers (London: Eyre & Spottiswoode, 1969), pp. 62–3.

40. C. J. Tyreman, *England and the Crusades 1095–1588* (University of Chicago Press, 1988), p. 247.

41. C. J. Tyreman, 'Philip VI and the recovery of the Holy Land', *EHR*, 100 (1985), 25–52, esp. 48.

42. M. C. E. Jones, 'Relations with France, 1337–1399', *England and her Neighbours*, p. 251; Vale, *Angevin Legacy*, p. 260.

43. This may be the purpose of the poem 'The Vows of the Heron', usually dated to the end of 1336; *Political Poems and Songs*, ed. T. Wright (London: Rolls Series, 1859), I, pp. 1–25, discussed in B. J. Whiting, 'The Vows of the Heron', *Speculum*, 20 (1945), 261–78.

44. Sumption, *Hundred Years War*, pp. 172–3; Jones, 'Relations with France', p. 243, on Philip VI's motives.

45. R. M. Haines, *Archbishop John Stratford* (Toronto: Pontifical Institute of Medieval Studies, 1986), p. 245; Lucas, *Low Countries*, p. 194; *Foedera*, II, iii, p. 165 (19 April 1337).

46. As cited in note 39 above.

47. *Chronicles*, pp. 57–60; Chaplais, 'Le Duché-pairie', p. 160.

48. Geoffrey Le Baker, *Chronicon*, ed. E. M. Thompson (1889), p. 61.

49. Chaplais, 'Le Duché-pairie', p. 160.

50. *Foedera*, II, iii, p. 192.

51. Déprez, *Préliminaires*, p. 191; *Foedera*, II, iv, pp. 24, 39, and passim for the years 1337 to 1339.

52. *Murimuth*, pp. 91–100, discussed in Déprez, *Préliminaires*, pp. 218–22.

53. H. S. Offler, 'England and Germany at the beginning of the Hundred Years War', *EHR*, 44 (1939), 608–31.

54. Lucas, *Low Countries*, pp. 358–60.

55. Ibid., pp. 362–3.

56. Ibid., p. 359, n. 175; *Le Bel*, I, pp. 167–8.

57. *Le Bel*, I, p. 168.

58. *Foedera*, II, iv, p. 64, given in *Avesbury*, p. 309, and taken seriously by Le Patourel, 'Edward III and the kingdom of France', pp. 180–2.

59. *Foedera*, II, iv, p. 83.

60. M. Prestwich, 'English Armies in the Early Stages of the Hundred Years War: a Scheme in 1341', *BIHR*, 56 (1983), 104–5.

61. *Rot. Parl.*, II, p. 113: *Oeuvres de Froissart*, ed. Kervyn de Lettenhove (1867–77, reprinted Osnabruk: Bibio Verlag, 1967), xviii, pp. 129–30.

Notes

62. *Foedera*, II, iv, p. 77.
63. *Murimuth*, pp. 116–19. On the political crisis in England in 1341 see Haines, *Archbishop John Stratford*, and the two recent studies of Edward III's reign, W. M. Ormrod, *The Reign of Edward III* (Yale University Press, 1990), and S. L. Waugh, *England in the Reign of Edward III* (Cambridge University Press, 1991).
64. Déprez, *Préliminaires*, pp. 337–42, 301–3.
65. J. J. N. Palmer, 'The War Aims of the Protagonists', in K. A. Fowler (ed.), *The Hundred Years War* (London: Macmillan, 1971), p. 52; Déprez, 'La Conférence d'Avignon', p. 307. See also Philip VI's reply to Edward's challenge of 27 July in *Murimuth*, pp. 112–14 and *Avesbury*, pp. 315–16.
66. *Le Bel*, pp. 167–8; Le Patourel, 'Edward III and the kingdom of France', p. 179.
67. *Le Bel*, p. 264, cited in M. C. E. Jones, 'The Breton Civil War' in *Froissart: Historian*, p. 75.
68. F. Bock, 'Some new documents illustrating the early years of the Hundred Years War (1353–56)', *Bulletin of the John Rylands Library*, 15 (1931), 61–70, 84–91. On the campaigns of Lancaster see K. A. Fowler, *The King's Lieutenant. Henry of Grosmont, first duke of Lancaster* (London: Elek Press, 1969).
69. W. M. Ormrod, 'Edward III and his family', *Journal of British Studies*, 27 (1987), 407–8 and appendix.
70. J. Le Patourel, 'Edward III "roi de France et duc de Normandie", 1356–60', *Revue historique de droit français et étranger*, 4e série, 31 (1953), 317–18.
71. *Chronicon Henrici Knighton*, ed. J. R. Lumby (London: Rolls Series, 1888–95), II, pp. 94–5.
72. R. Cazelles, *Société politique, noblesse et couronne sous Jean le Bon et Charles V* (Geneva and Paris: Droz, 1982), pp. 126–8.
73. Ibid., pp. 189–93, 211, 213–17.
74. On French reactions to defeat see F. Autrand, 'La déconfiture. La bataille de Poitiers (1356) à travers quelques textes français des XIV et XV siècles', in *Guerre et Société*, pp. 93–121.
75. J. Horeau-Dodineau, 'Les fondements des préférences dynastiques au XIVe siècle d'après quelques lettres de remission' in *La France Anglaise*, pp. 113–21; W. M. Ormrod, 'The double monarchy of Edward III', *Medieval History*, 1 (1991), 74.
76. Bock, 'Some new documents', pp. 70–83, 91–6.
77. J. Le Patourel, 'The Treaty of Brétigny, 1360', *TRHS*, 5th series 10 (1960), 19–39. The text of the first does not survive, the second

is printed in E. Cosneau, *Les Grands traités de la Guerre de Cent Ans* (Paris: Picard, 1889), pp. 3–32.

78. Le Patourel, 'Treaty', p. 30, where he calls the second Treaty of London 'preposterous'.

79. Cosneau, *Grands traités*, pp. 33–68; *English Historical Documents*, IV, pp. 103–8.

80. P. Chaplais, 'Some documents regarding the fulfilment and interpretation of the Treaty of Brétigny', *Camden Miscellany XIX* (London: Camden Society, 80, 1952), 6.

81. This is essentially Le Patourel's conclusion in 'Treaty', pp. 38–9.

82. *Rot. Parl.*, II, p. 135 (1343, when included with Wales, Ireland, Scotland and Flanders: Brittany was included in 1344 and 1350 (pp. 146, 226)); Chaplais, 'Chancery of Guyenne', p. 83.

83. Chaplais, 'Some documents', p. 8, well summarised in Jones, 'Relations with France', p. 253.

84. In the creation of the Black Prince as prince of Aquitaine 19 July 1362, *Foedera*, III, ii, p. 66.

85. Ibid., pp. 66–8 (1362), III, iii, p. 5 (1373).

86. *Rot. Parl.*, II, p. 276.

87. For what follows see J. J. N. Palmer, 'England, France, the papacy and the Flemish succession', *Journal of Medieval History*, 2 (1976), pp. 339–64.

88. P. E. Russell, *The English Intervention in Spain and Portugal in the time of Edward III and Richard II* (Oxford: Clarendon Press, 1955), pp. xxi–xxii and chapters 3–7 on the Black Prince's policies.

89. P. Morgan, *War and Society in Medieval Cheshire 1277–1403* (Manchester: Chetham Society third series 34, 1987), pp. 121–36.

90. *Foedera*, III, ii, pp. 148–50.

91. Ibid., p. 157.

92. J. J. N. Palmer, *England, France and Christendom, 1377–99* (London: Routledge, 1972), pp. 1–2.

93. *Foedera*, III, ii, p. 151.

94. Ibid, pp. 159 (June), 166 (December).

95. Palmer, *England, France*, p. 1. For discussion of the size, composition and cost of armies in this period see J. W. Sherborne, 'Indentured retinues and English expeditions to France 1369–89', *EHR*, 79 (1964), 718–46, and his 'The cost of English warfare with France in the later fourteenth century', *BIHR*, 50 (1977), 135–50.

96. J. W. Sherborne, 'The battle of La Rochelle and the war at sea, 1372–75', *BIHR*, 42 (1969), 17–29.

97. *Foedera*, III, ii, pp. 158–9, 161.
98. For what follows see M. C. E. Jones, *Ducal Brittany 1364–1399* (Oxford: Clarendon Press, 1970). He points out (pp. 78 and 90) that seven major and two minor expeditions between 1370 and 1380 involved Brittany or Duke John IV.
99. Sherborne, 'Battle of La Rochelle', p. 23.
100. E. Perroy, 'The Anglo-French negotiations at Bruges', *Camden Miscellany XIX* (London: Camden Society, 1952), xvi–xvii, 11, 38, 43, 53–5.
101. There is a useful discussion of the 1377 raids on southern England in E. Searle and R. Burghart, 'The defense of England and the Peasants' Revolt', *Viator*, 3 (1972), 365–88.
102. J. A. Tuck, 'Richard II and the Hundred Years War', in *Politics and Crisis in Fourteenth-Century England*, ed. J. Taylor and W. Childs (Gloucester: Alan Sutton, 1990), p. 122.
103. *Rot. Parl.*, III, p. 36.
104. J. W. Sherborne, 'The costs of English warfare with France', p. 149.
105. Palmer, *England, France*, p. 9.
106. Ibid., pp. 21–4 and appendix 2.
107. J. W. Sherborne, 'The Defence of the Realm and the Impeachment of Michael de la Pole in 1386', in *Politics and Crisis*, p. 98.
108. This is Palmer's view in 'The Last Summons of the Feudal Levy in England (1385)', *EHR*, 83 (1968), 771–5, but see also N. B. Lewis, 'The last medieval summons of the English feudal levy, 13 June 1385', *EHR*, 68 (1958), 1–26 and his 'Feudal summons of 1385', *EHR*, 100 (1985), 726–43, with Palmer's reply, pp. 743–6.
109. J. S. Roskell, *The Impeachment of Michael de la Pole, Earl of Suffolk, in 1386 in the context of the reign of Richard II* (Manchester University Press, 1984), p. 45.
110. Sherborne, 'Defence of the Realm', p. 115.
111. Palmer, *England, France*, p. 68.
112. S. Armitage-Smith, *John of Gaunt* (London: Constable, 1904), pp. 330–2.
113. *Foedera*, III, iv, p. 39 (18 June) subsequently extended to 1398.
114. Tuck, 'Richard II and the Hundred Years War', p. 125.
115. *Foedera*, III, iv, pp. 53–4; *Rot. Parl.*, III, pp. 263–4.
116. Palmer, *England, France*, chapters 8 and 9. This line is also followed by Allmand, *Hundred Years War*, pp. 25–6.
117. J. J. N. Palmer, 'Articles for a final peace between England and France, 16 June 1393', *BIHR*, 39 (1966), 180–5, and 'The

Anglo-French peace negotiations, 1390–1396', *TRHS*, 5th series, 16 (1966), 81–94.

118. Palmer, *England, France*, pp. 159–63; 'Anglo-French peace negotiations 1390–1396', p. 85.

119. Review of Palmer's *England, France and Christendom* in *EHR*, 88 (1973), 848–53.

120. Vale, *English Gascony 1399–1453* (Oxford: Clarendon Press, 1970), p. 32, esp. n.4, and p. 33.

121. Tuck, 'Richard II and the Hundred Years War', pp. 127–8; *The Westminster Chronicle 1381–1394*, ed. L. C. Hector and B. F. Harvey (Oxford: Clarendon Press, 1982), pp. 516–18; *Rot. Parl.*, III, pp. 315–16.

122. C. J. Phillpotts, 'John of Gaunt and English policy towards France 1389–95', *Journal of Medieval History*, 16 (1990), 363–86.

123. C. J. Phillpotts, 'English policy towards France during the truces 1389–1417', unpub. PhD thesis, University of Liverpool, 1985, p. 30.

124. See, for instance, Richard's letter to the duchy of 7 July 1392, *Proceedings and Ordinances of the Privy Council*, ed. N. H. Nicolas (London: Record Commission, 1834–7), I, p. 79.

125. *Westminster Chronicle*, p. 518; *Eulogium Historiarum*, III, ed. F. S. Haydon (London: Rolls Series, 1863), p. 369.

126. *Oeuvres*, XV, pp. 135–6, 147–69.

127. L. D. Duls, *Richard II in the Early Chronicles* (The Hague and Paris: Mouton, 1975), pp. 87–8.

128. Palmer, *England, France*, p. 166.

129. Ibid., pp. 169–70

130. *Foedera*, III, iv. pp. 115–17, also printed in Cosneau, *Grands traités*, pp. 69–99.

131. See Palmer, *England, France*, chapter 12 on Richard's hardline approach to the French and Germans after the truce.

132. For example in March 1397, *Proceedings and Ordinances of the Privy Council*, I, p. 64, although on other occasions the title 'adversary of France' was used.

3   NEW WARS OR OLD? ANGLO-FRENCH CONFLICT IN THE
FIFTEENTH CENTURY

1. Duls, *Richard II in the Early Chronicles*, p. 131, n. 46.

2. *Foedera*, IV, i, pp. 85–7 (Aug.–Sept. 1405) as a result of Glendower's treaty with France, 14 July 1404 (p. 69). Except for the

period from December 1419 to October 1422 no English ruler was formally recognised by the valois as king of England from the usurpation of Henry IV to the negotiations of 1474–5 (*Foedera*, V, iii, p. 67).

3. Froissart, *Oeuvres*, XVI, pp. 189–90, 211–12.
4. Vale, *English Gascony*, pp. 29–31. On French policy in general see Palmer, *England, France*, p. 225.
5. S. P. Pistono, 'Henry IV and Charles VI; the confirmation of the twenty-eight year truce', *Journal of Medieval History*, 3 (1977), 357.
6. *Proceedings and Ordinances of the Privy Council*, I, pp. 143–4.
7. J. L. Kirby, *Henry IV* (London: Constable) provides the best narrative, esp. pp. 124, 161, 163 and 171.
8. J. L. Kirby, 'The siege of Bourg, 1406', *History Today*, 18 (1968), 60.
9. *Foedera*, IV, i, p. 109.
10. *Rot. Parl.*, III, pp. 574–5 (June 1406), 581–2 (reversal in December). For a different explanation of these events see Kirby, *Henry IV*, p. 205.
11. Perroy, *Hundred Years War*, p. 213.
12. *Foedera*, IV, i, p. 148.
13. *Rot. Parl.*, III, p. 427, and the previous page for the homage for his English lands.
14. Ibid., p. 656–7; *Foedera*, IV, ii, p. 5.
15. R. Vaughan, *John the Fearless* (London: Longman, 1966), p. 92; *Monstrelet*, II, p. 189.
16. *Foedera*, IV, ii, pp. 12–13 (printed in part in *English Historical Documents*, IV, pp. 204–5) and p. 4 for the January approach.
17. Ibid., p. 15; Vale, *English Gascony*, pp. 58–63. Ex info. John Milner, who presented a paper on the expedition to a colloquium at Manchester in July 1989.
18. See Walsingham's judgement that Henry IV could have recovered his rights in France 'if the strength of his body had equalled the strength of his spirit', *St Albans Chronicle, 1406–1420*, ed. V. H. Galbraith (Oxford: Clarendon Press, 1937), p. 64.
19. Le Patourel, 'Treaty of Brétigny', p. 39.
20. For the demands of this embassy see *Foedera*, IV, ii, pp. 106–9. Henry had previously ordered preparation of materials on the Brétigny settlement, ibid., p. 84.
21. *Foedera*, IV, ii, p. 107.
22. Jouvenal des Ursins, *Histoire de Charles VI*, ed. D. Godefroy (Paris, 1653), p. 289.

23. Vale, *English Gascony*, pp. 72–4.
24. The author of the *Gesta Henrici Quinti*, pp. 58–9, suggests that only 5900 men were left on the march to Calais, other English chronicles giving slightly higher figures. I am currently examining the surviving muster rolls and accounts with a view to establishing a more reliable figure.
25. C. T. Allmand, *Lancastrian Normandy, 1415–1450* (Oxford: Clarendon Press, 1983), chapters 3 and 4; R. A. Massey, 'The Land Settlement in Lancastrian Normandy', *Property and Politics: Essays in Later Medieval English History* (Gloucester: Alan Sutton, 1984), pp. 76–96.
26. R. A. Newhall, 'Henry V's policy of conciliation in Normandy 1417–1422', *Anniversary Essays in Medieval History of Students of C. H. Haskins*, ed C. H. Taylor (Harvard University Press, 1929).
27. Thomas Walsingham, *Ypodigma Neustriae*, ed. H. T. Riley (London: Rolls Series, 1876).
28. Allmand, *Lancastrian Normandy*, pp. 124–6.
29. A. E. Curry, 'Le Service féodal en Normandie de 1417 à 1450', in *La France Anglaise*, pp. 233–57.
30. This conclusion is derived from a study of Bibliothèque Nationale manuscrits français 26042 and 26043.
31. The fullest account is provided in R. A. Newhall, *The English Conquest of Normandy 1416–1424* (Yale University Press, 1924).
32. *Foedera*, IV, iii, p. 126. For earlier negotiations see ibid., pp. 68–74 (with Dauphin, October 1418) and *Le Fèvre*, I, p. 348 (with Burgundy, spring 1419).
33. *Foedera*, IV, iii, p. 125; *Waurin*, II, p. 272.
34. J. Shirley, *A Parisian Journal, 1405–1449* (Oxford: Clarendon Press, 1968), p. 138.
35. *Foedera*, IV, iii, pp. 128–9.
36. See, for instance, *St. Albans Chronicle*, p. 124.
37. P. Bonenfant, *Du meutre de Montereau au traité de Troyes* (Brussels: Académie Royale de Belgique, 1958).
38. *Chronique du Religieux de Saint Denis*, vi, pp. 376–7.
39. Bonenfant, *Du meutre*, annexe 3.
40. Ibid., annexe 4.
41. *Foedera*, IV, iii, p. 135 (1 Oct.); *Proceedings and Ordinances of the Privy Council*, II, p. 269.
42. Bonenfant, *Du meutre*, annexe 7.
43. *Foedera*, IV, iii, pp. 140–1.
44. *Journal de Clément de Fauquemberge, greffier du Parlement de*

Paris, 1417–35, ed. A. Tuetey (Paris: Société de l'Histoire de France, 1903–15), I, p. 361.

45. Cosneau, *Grands traités*, pp. 100–15; *English Historical Documents*, IV, pp. 225–6 gives only extracts from the treaty.
46. See, for instance, for French opinion, *Waurin*, II, p. 299, *Monstrelet*, III, p. 379, *Le Fèvre*, I, p. 384, and for English, *The Chronicle of John Hardyng*, ed. H. Ellis (London, 1812), p. 379. *Political Poems and Songs*, II, pp. 131, 141.
47. C. A. J. Armstrong, 'La double monarchie France-Angleterre et la maison de Bourgogne', *Annales de Bourgogne*, 37 (1965) pp. 81–2, 87.
48. B. P. Wolffe, *Henry VI* (London: Eyre Methuen, 1981), pp. 60–2, where the alleged Englishness of the ceremony is discussed.
49. *Foedera*, IV, iii, p. 194.
50. *Journal de Clément de Fauquembergue*, II, p. 65 and the 'Traité compendieux de la querelle de France contre les anglois' cited in P. S. Lewis, *Later Medieval France: the Polity* (London: Macmillan, 1968), p. 95, n. 2.
51. There are two excellent studies of Charles VII: M. G. A. Vale, *Charles VII* (London: Eyre Methuen, 1974); R. G. Little, *The Parlement of Poitiers. War, Government and Politics in France 1418–36* (London: Royal Historical Society, 1984).
52. Vale, *English Gascony*, pp. 80–1.
53. J. Dickinson, *The Congress of Arras, 1435* (Oxford: Clarendon Press, 1955), p. 14: *Chronique du Religieux de Saint Denis*, VI, pp. 438–9.
54. The form of oath is given in a document dated the same day as the treaty, *Foedera*, IV, iii, p. 174. The Bourgeois of Paris (*Parisian Journal*, p. 185) comments on the oath taking of 1423, saying that 'some were glad to do it, others most reluctant'.
55. B. J. H. Rowe, 'The Grand Conseil under the duke of Bedford', in *Essays in Medieval History Presented to H. E. Salter* (Oxford: Clarendon Press, 1934), pp. 207–34. There is a useful recent study of Paris: G. L. Thompson, *Paris and its People under English Rule: the Anglo-Burgundian Regime 1420–1436* (Oxford: Clarendon Press, 1991).
56. *Monstrelet*, IV, p. 110; *Proceedings and Ordinances of the Privy Council*, III, p. 248.
57. There are two fine studies of the reign of Henry VI; B. P. Wolffe, *Henry VI* (London: Eyre Methuen, 1981) and R. A. Griffiths, *The Reign of Henry VI* (Tonbridge: Benn, 1981).
58. There is no full narrative in English of this period of the war. What follows is derived from my own study of documents con-

cerning the administration of the English army in France. See also A. J. Pollard, *John Talbot and the War in France 1427–1453* (London: Royal Historical Society, 1983).

59. M. H. Keen, 'The End of the Hundred Years War: Lancastrian France and Lancastrian England', in *England and Her Neighbours*, pp. 310–11.

60. Allmand, *Lancastrian Normandy*, pp. 33–4, 235.

61. For a detailed study of York's two periods of office see P. A. Johnson, *Duke Richard of York, 1411–1461* (Oxford: Clarendon Press, 1988).

62. There is a useful summary in Allmand, *Lancastrian Normandy*, pp. 273–8.

63. Keen, 'End of the Hundred Years War', p. 302.

64. C. T. Allmand, 'The Anglo-French Negotiations, 1439', *BIHR*, 40 (1967), 1–33, and his 'Documents Relating to the Anglo-French negotiations of 1439', *Camden Miscellany XXIV* (London: Royal Historical Society, 1972).

65. *Foedera*, V, i, pp. 133–5. The best account of the diplomacy of the 1440s is provided by Wolffe, *Henry VI*, chapters 10 and 11.

66. M. K. Jones, 'John Beaufort, Duke of Somerset and the French Expedition of 1443', in *Patronage, Crown and the Provinces in Later Medieval England*, ed. R. A. Griffiths (Gloucester: Alan Sutton, 1981), pp. 75–102.

67. For the financial problems of the truce period see G. L. Harriss, 'Marmaduke Lumley and the Exchequer Crisis of 1446–9', in *Aspects of Late Medieval Government and Society. Essays Presented to J. R. Lander*, ed. J. G. Rowe (Toronto: 1986), pp. 143–78.

68. M. J. Daniel and M. H. Keen, 'English diplomacy and the sack of Fougères', *History*, 59 (1974), 374–91.

69. A. E. Curry, 'Towns at war: Norman towns under English rule, 1417–1450' in *Towns and Townspeople in the Fifteenth century*, ed. J. A. Thomson (Gloucester: Alan Sutton, 1989), pp. 148–72.

70. Wolffe, *Henry VI*, pp. 265–6, 270, 273–4; Pollard, *John Talbot*, pp. 134–8, M. G. A. Vale, 'The last days of English Gascony 1451–1453', *TRHS*, 5th series 19 (1969), 119–38.

71. P. D. Solon, 'Valois military administration on the Norman frontier 1445–61: a study in medieval reform', *Speculum*, 51 (1976), 91–111; Griffiths, *Reign of Henry VI*, pp. 814–16.

72. Vale, *Charles VII*, p. 155.

73. Wolffe, *Henry VI*, p. 276. See also the excellent discussion in M. K. Jones, 'Somerset, York and the Wars of the Roses', *EHR*, 104 (1989), 285–307.

74. J. A. Ferguson, *English Diplomacy 1422–1461* (Oxford: Clarendon Press, 1972), p. 33.
75. G. L. Harriss, 'The struggle for Calais. An aspect of the rivalry between Lancaster and York', *EHR*, 75 (1960), 52.
76. C. D. Ross, *Edward IV* (London: Eyre Methuen, 1975), pp. 159–60.
77. S. B. Chrimes, *Henry VII* (London: Eyre Methuen, 1972), p. 37.
78. PRO E30/534, cited in *List and Index XLIX* (London: HMSO, 1923), p. 53.
79. Ross, *Edward IV*, pp. 111–14, and chapter 9.
80. J. R. Lander, 'The Hundred Years War and Edward IV's 1475 campaign in France' in *Tudor Men and Institutions*, ed. A. J. Slavin (Louisiana State University Press, 1972), pp. 70–100, reprinted in his *Crown and Nobility 1450–1509* (London: Arnold, 1976), pp. 220–41; *Literae Cantuariensis*, ed. J. B. Sheppard (London: Rolls Series, 1887–9), III, pp. 274–85.
81. Ross, *Edward IV*, pp. 223–33.
82. Lander, '1475 campaign', pp. 93–100.
83. Chrimes, *Henry VII*, pp. 280–2.
84. *Foedera*, V, iv, pp. 48–50 for the advice of the captains, and pp. 52–4 for the agreement at Etaples. For similar advice put to Edward IV in 1475 see V, iii, p. 65.
85. Chrimes, *Henry VII*, p. 36.
86. Gunn, 'French wars of Henry VIII', pp. 28–51. It is also interesting that Edward IV copied materials on Lancastrian Normandy although his purpose is unclear, W. F. Jordan, *The Chronicle and Political Papers of King Edward IV* (London: Allen and Unwin, 1966), pp. xxi–xxxiii, 185–90.
87. 'Introduction' to *Henry VIII. A European Court in England*, ed. D. Starkey (London: National Maritime Museum, 1991), p. 12, and, in the same volume, C. Giry-Deloison, 'A Diplomatic Revolution? Anglo-French Relations and the Treaty of 1527', p. 77.
88. S. J. Gunn, 'The Duke of Suffolk's march on Paris 1523', *EHR*, 101 (1986), 629.
89. Giry-Deloison, 'Diplomatic Revolution?', pp. 77–83.
90. Cited in R. B. Wernham, *The Making of English Foreign Policy 1558–1603* (University of California Press, 1980), p. 1. See also P. Gwyn's view in 'Wolsey's Foreign Policy: the conferences at Calais and Bruges', *Historical Journal*, 23 (1980), 757, on the rationale behind the meeting of Francis I and Henry in the Field of the Cloth of Gold, 1520: 'to remove the prejudices built up over at least two hundred years of enmity, something out of the

ordinary was necessary, something, as it were, that could outshine Agincourt'.

91. H. F. Chettle, 'The Burgesses for Calais 1536–58', *EHR*, 50 (1935), 493.

4 THE WIDER CONTEXT

1. In addition to the papacy and the empire, the kingdoms of England, France, Scotland, Castile, Aragon, Portugal, Navarre and Bohemia; the duchies of Burgundy, Brittany, Brabant and Luxembourg; the counties of Flanders, Hainault (with Holland and Zeeland), Bar, Savoy, Milan, Guelders, Namur, Nassau, Juliers, Namur and Palatine; the archbishoprics of Cologne, Münster and Liège; the commune of Genoa.

2. Cosneau, *Grands traités*, pp. 53–5, 60 (Brétigny), 96 (1396).

3. Ibid., pp. 79 and 81.

4. Déprez, *Préliminaires*, p. 341.

5. W. Childs, *Anglo-Castilian Trade in the later Middle Ages* (Manchester University Press, 1978), pp. 24–5, 28, 43.

6. Russell, *English Intervention*, pp. xxi–xxiii.

7. R. Vaughan, *Philip the Good* (London: Longmans, 1970), pp. 31–50.

8. Ormrod, 'Edward III and his family', pp. 398–422.

9. In the 1330s and 40s, Lucas, *Low Countries*, chapters 8–10; in the 1380s, Palmer, *England, France*, pp. 45–7.

10. For the fifteenth century, see J. Ferguson, *English Diplomacy 1422–1461* (Oxford: Clarendon Press, 1972). There is no similar overview for the fourteenth century, but Sumption's *Hundred Years War* is useful for 1337–46.

11. *Foedera*, III, ii, pp. 148–50.

12. Ferguson, *English Diplomacy*, p. xxiv. There are few general surveys of late medieval Europe. See D. Hay, *Europe in the Fourteenth and Fifteenth Centuries* (second edition, London: Longman, 1989) and D. J. A. Matthew, *An Atlas of Medieval Europe* (London: Phaidon Press, 1983).

13. These are well elucidated in Lucas, *Low Countries*, and in H. Offler, 'England and Germany at the beginning of the Hundred Years War', *EHR*, 44 (1939), 608–31.

14. R. Vaughan has charted the accretion of power in his biographies of the four Valois dukes, all published by Longman Press: *Philip the Bold* (1963), *John the Fearless* (1966), *Philip the Good* (1970)

and *Charles the Bold* (1973), and in *Valois Burgundy* (London: Allen Lane, 1976).

15. M. G. A. Vale, 'The Anglo-French Wars 1294–1340: Allies and Alliances', in *Guerre et Société en France, en Angleterre et en Bourgogne XIVe–XVe siècle*, ed. P. Contamine, C. Giry-Deloison, M. H. Keen (Lille: Université de Charles de Gaulle, 1991), pp. 15–31.

16. Ferguson, *English Diplomacy*, pp. 59, 71 (Henry V); 62, 69, 74, 95–6 (Henry VI).

17. A. Rucquoi, 'Français et Castillans: une "internationale chévaleresque"' in *La France Anglaise*, p. 419. A useful overview of English relations with Spain is provided by A. Goodman, 'England and Iberia in the Middle Ages', in *England and her Neighbours*, pp. 73–96.

18. J. H. Munro, 'An economic aspect of the collapse of the Anglo-Burgundian alliance, 1428–1442', *EHR*, 75 (1970), 225–44.

19. Childs, *Anglo-Castilian Trade*, pp. 32–3, 40–2.

20. Lucas, *Low Countries*, p. 214.

21. J. L. Bolton, *The Medieval English Economy 1150–1500* (London: Dent, 1980), pp. 298–300.

22. J. Le Patourel, 'The King and the Princes in Fourteenth Century France', in *Europe in the Later Middle Ages*, ed. J. R. Hale, R. Highfield and B. Smalley (London: Faber and Faber, 1965), p. 183.

23. Vaughan, *Valois Burgundy*, chapter 7.

24. Clause 26, Cosneau, *Grands traités*, p. 112.

25. Vale, *English Gascony*, p. 96; Jouvenal des Ursins, *Histoire de Charles VI*, p. 382.

26. See, for instance, the comments of the English ambassadors in 1344 (Déprez, 'Conference d'Avignon', p. 313).

27. Cuttino, *English Diplomatic Administration, 1259–1339* (second edn, Oxford: Clarendon Press, 1971), p. 187. There is a fascinating collection of texts in P. Chaplais (ed.), *English Medieval Diplomatic Practice: Part I*, 2 vols (London: HMSO, 1982).

28. *English Historical Documents*, iv, pp. 62–3; *Gesta Henrici Quinti*, p. 9.

29. Chaplais, *English Medieval Diplomatic Practice*, I, i, pp. 205–6, 210–13.

30. Fowler, 'Truces', in *The Hundred Years War*, ed. K. A. Fowler (London: Macmillan, 1976), pp. 184–215.

31. F. R. H. Du Boulay, *Germany in the Later Middle Ages* (London: Athlone Press, 1983), pp. 26–9. Philip VI (D. Wood, *Clement VI*

(Cambridge: University Press, 1989) pp. 126–7, Edward III (Offler, 'England and Germany', pp. 628–30), Charles VI (Palmer, *England, France*, p. 192) and Richard II (ibid., pp. 212, 218) all toyed with advancing their own imperial candidature.

32. Wood, *Clement VI*, p. 127.
33. These aspects, and the impact of the schism, are discussed in P. Heath, *Church and Realm, 1272–1461* (London: Fontana, 1988). For Anglo-papal relations in the fifteenth century see Ferguson, *English Diplomacy*, chapter VII.
34. These conclusions are derived from a reading of Déprez, *Preliminaires*, esp. pp. 337–42, and Wood, *Clement VI*, chapter 6.
35. J. Campbell, 'England, Scotland and the Hundred Years War', in *Europe in the Later Middle Ages*, p. 187. This line is followed by A. Grant, *Independence and Nationhood. Scotland 1306–1469* (London: Edward Arnold, 1984), p. 22.
36. For a general appraisal of English overlordship before and after 1290 see R. Frame, *The Political Development of the British Isles 1100–1400* (Oxford University Press, 1990).
37. M. Prestwich, 'England and Scotland during the Wars of Independence', in *England and her Neighbours*, p. 183.
38. G. S. Barrow, *Robert Bruce* (third edition, Edinburgh University Press, 1988), pp. 49–59.
39. J. Green, 'Anglo-Scottish Relations 1160–1174', in *England and her Neighbours*, p. 69.
40. Prestwich, 'England and Scotland', p. 185.
41. A. A. M. Duncan, *The Nation of Scots and the Declaration of Arbroath (1320)* (London: Historical Association G75, 1970), pp. 34–7 for the text.
42. Ibid., pp. 28–9.
43. Nicholson, *Edward III and the Scots*, p. 51.
44. Ibid., chapters 5 and 6.
45. Ibid., p. 76.
46. *Rot. Parl.*, II, p. 67.
47. *Foedera*, II, iii, p. 97.
48. *Foedera*, II, iii, p. 115.
49. *Scalacronica*, trans. H. Maxwell (Glasgow: Maclehose, 1907), p. 93.
50. *Grandes Chroniques*, IX, p. 143.
51. M. McKisack, *The Fourteenth Century* (Oxford: Clarendon Press, 1959), p. 118.
52. Nicholson, *Edward III and the Scots*, pp. 192–3, 217.

53. Déprez, *Préliminaires*, p. 123.
54. *Foedera*, II, iii, p. 187. See also *Grandes Chroniques*, IX, p. 158 for the view that Edward involved himself on the continent in response to events in Scotland.
55. Prestwich, 'England and Scotland', p. 197.
56. Campbell, 'England, Scotland and the Hundred Years War', pp. 186, 191, 194–5 on the costs of the Scottish front 1337–8.
57. Déprez, 'Conférence d'Avignon', p. 312.
58. For a letter from Philip to David urging invasion see Campbell, 'England, Scotland and the Hundred Years War', p. 195.
59. Details of negotiations for David's release are given in Grant, *Independence and Nationhood*, pp. 35–7.
60. *Regesta Regum Scottorum VI. The Acts of David II*, ed. B. Webster (Edinburgh University Press, 1982), pp. 184–91. On the 1356 campaign see Campbell, 'England, Scotland and the Hundred Years War', p. 200.
61. *Foedera*, III, ii, pp. 161–3.
62. Grant, *Independence and Nationhood*, p. 40.
63. Campbell, 'England, Scotland and the Hundred Years War', pp. 192–3.
64. Grant, *Independence and Nationhood*, pp. 42–3; Palmer, *England, France*, pp. 173, 213. On Scottish government after 1357 see B. Webster, 'David II and the government of fourteenth-century Scotland', *TRHS*, 5th series 16 (1966), 116–20.
65. For Henry V see P. J. Bradley, 'Henry V's Scottish policy: a study in realpolitik', in *Documenting the Past*, pp. 177–95.
66. There is an excellent study by B. G. H. Ditcham, 'The employment of foreign mercenary troops in French royal armies 1415–70', PhD thesis, University of Edinburgh (1978).
67. Grant, *Independence and Nationhood*, pp. 50–1.
68. Cited in R. B. Wernham, *Before the Armada. The Growth of English Foreign Policy 1485–1588* (London: Cape, 1966), p. 240.
69. Froissart, *Chronicles*, pp. 46–54; see also Le Bel, I, p. 41, noting his comments on the barrenness of Northumberland.

CONCLUSION

1. The remark was made by John Gummer during a working lunch with the French Agriculture Minister on Friday, 26 June 1992 (*Daily Telegraph*, 27 June, p. 5). In this newspaper's report, a cartoon from *Le Monde* on the dispute between French and

English fishermen was also reproduced. The cartoon featured two ships; on one, British fishermen were shouting 'French bastards' ('enfoirés de Français'), on the other French fishermen responded with 'English drunkards' ('empaffés d'Anglais'). In the water a fish declared 'long live Maastricht ('vive Maastricht'), a reference to the treaty on European unity which was at this point still to be ratified. The terms of abuse have a pedigree which stretches back to the Hundred Years War. As for the fish, it was popularly rumoured that so many Frenchmen fell into the water at the English naval victory at Sluys in 1340 that if the fish could have spoken they would have learned French!

SELECT BIBLIOGRAPHY

This bibliography is highly selective, listing only the major books and articles relevant to the themes covered in this book. It confines itself largely to works in English which should easily be accessible through educational or public library services. Further materials, usually those of a more specialised nature, are cited in the references for each chapter. Guides to contemporary sources and to the historiography of the war are provided in the references to chapter 1. A fuller bibliography is provided in Allmand's *Hundred Years War*, but for details of recent works one should consult the Royal Historical Society's annual *Bibliography of British and Irish History*, and the twice-yearly *International Medieval Bibliography* produced at the University of Leeds.

C. T. Allmand, *Lancastrian Normandy. The History of a Medieval Occupation 1415–50* (Oxford: Clarendon Press, 1983). A full investigation which emphasises the significance of Normandy to English interests.

C. T. Allmand, *The Hundred Years War* (Cambridge University Press, 1988). A stimulating and wide-ranging study which considers the implications of the conflict from both the English and French viewpoints.

P. Chaplais, 'English arguments concerning the feudal status of Aquitaine in the fourteenth century', *BIHR*, 21 (1946–8). Demonstrates Edward I's attempts to circumvent the Treaty of Paris of 1259.

P. Chaplais, *Essays in Medieval Diplomacy and Administration* (London: Hambledon Press, 1981). A reprint of most of Chaplais' highly valuable articles on the problem of Gascony and other issues relating to the wars, all emphasising the difficulties inherent in English tenure of lands in France.

P. Contamine, *War in the Middle Ages* (first pub. in French 1980, Engl. edn trans. M. C. E. Jones, Oxford: Blackwell, 1984). A magisterial review with an excellent bibliography.

P. Contamine, C. Giry-Deloison and M. H. Keen (eds), *Guerre et Société en France, en Angleterre et en Bourgogne XIVe–XVe siècle* (Lille: Université de Charles de Gaulle, 1991). A collection of articles which reveals the in-depth documentary study currently being carried out on both sides of the Channel

G. P. Cuttino, *English Diplomatic Administration 1259–1339* (Oxford: Clarendon Press, 1940, second edn 1971). Includes an important study of attempts to reach a settlement in the early fourteenth century.

G. P. Cuttino, 'Historical revision: the causes of the Hundred Years War', *Speculum*, 31 (1956), 463–77. A review of the historiography from 1899 to 1956.

E. Déprez, *Les Préliminaires de la Guerre de Cent Ans* (Paris, 1902, Geneva: Slatkine-Megariotis Reprints, 1975). Old but still valuable because of its extensive quotations from primary sources.

J. Dickinson, *The Congress of Arras 1435* (Oxford: Clarendon Press, 1955). A detailed study of the events which led to Burgundian defection to the French.

J. Ferguson, *English Diplomacy 1422–1461* (Oxford: Clarendon Press, 1972). Examines Anglo-French diplomacy as well as England's dealings with other European states.

K. A. Fowler, *The Age of Plantagenet and Valois* (London: Elek Press, 1967). A coffee-table book in terms of its presentation but with an excellent text; perhaps the most satisfying and most readable book on the subject.

K. A. Fowler, *The King's Lieutenant. Henry of Grosmont, first duke of Lancaster* (London: Elek Press, 1969). Much more than a biography, and particularly useful on English policies in the 1340s and 50s.

K. A. Fowler (ed.), *The Hundred Years War* (London: Macmillan, 1971). A valuable collection of essays written by specialists on different subjects. The articles by Le Patourel ('Origins') and Palmer ('War Aims of the Protagonists') provide straightforward yet challenging introductions to these topics.

La France Anglaise au Moyen Age. Actes du 111e Congrès des Sociétés Savantes, Poitiers 1986 (Paris: CTHS, 1988). Research papers presented by French and English historians at a conference devoted to English interests in France.

R. A. Griffiths, *The Reign of Henry VI* (London: Ernest Benn, 1981). An extremely thorough and extensively referenced study of the reign which gives considerable attention to English enterprises in France.

G. L. Harriss, *King, Parliament and Public Finance in England to 1369* (Oxford: Clarendon Press, 1975). A full account of how Edward raised money for his wars, and the implications this had for the development of English government and parliament.

G. L. Harriss, *Cardinal Beaufort. A Study of Lancastrian Ascendancy and Decline* (Oxford: Clarendon Press, 1988). Contains much of interest on the problems of war finance and on the formulation of English policy towards France in the post-Troyes period.

M. C. E. Jones, *Ducal Brittany 1364–1399* (Oxford: Clarendon Press, 1970). Gives due emphasis to the role of Brittany and its duke in English war policies in the later fourteenth century.

M. C. E. Jones and M. G. A. Vale, *England and her Neighbours 1066–1453. Essays in Honour of Pierre Chaplais* (London: Hambledon Press, 1989). Contains not only Vale's review of the historiography of the Hundred Years War but also important articles by Keen on the end of Lancastrian France and by Jones on Anglo-French relations in the fourteenth century. Other articles on England's relations with Scotland, Spain and Germany help to set the Hundred Years War firmly in its European context.

M. K. Jones, 'Somerset, York and the Wars of the Roses', *EHR*, 104 (1989), 285–307. Comes to important conclusions on the links between failure in France and the origins of civil war in England.

M. H. Keen, *England in the Later Middle Ages* (London: Eyre Methuen, 1977). The best text book on the period.

J. Le Patourel, 'Edward III and the kingdom of France', *History*, 43 (1958), 173–89. A seminal article, significant because it gave more credence than usual to Edward's ambitions for the French crown.

J. Le Patourel, 'The Treaty of Brétigny 1360', *TRHS*, 5th series 10 (1960), 19–39. A highly influential study of this treaty.

H. S. Lucas, *The Low Countries and the Hundred Years War 1326–47* (University of Michigan, 1929, reprinted Philadelphia: Porcupine Press, 1976). A very detailed study which emphasises the role of Flanders and the rest of the Low Countries in the origins of the Hundred Years War.

R. A. Massey, 'The Land Settlement in Lancastrian Normandy', in *Property and Politics: Essays in Later Medieval English History*, ed. A. J. Pollard (Gloucester: Alan Sutton, 1984), pp. 76–96. An analysis of this important aspect of English policy in France.

P. Morgan, *War and Society in Medieval Cheshire 1277–1403* (Manchester: Chetham Society, third series, 34, 1987). A novel approach, which considers the wars of the later middle ages through the experiences of the men of one county.

R. A. Newhall, *The English Conquest of Normandy 1416-24* (Yale University Press, 1924). A detailed account of these campaigns.

W. M. Ormrod, *The Reign of Edward III* (Yale University Press 1990). Not a full biography as such but a study which clearly reveals the significance of war to Edward's kingship and to the political nation.

J. J. N. Palmer, *England, France and Christendom, 1377-99* (London: Routledge, 1972). A controversial study of English war policies in the time of Richard II.

J. J. N. Palmer, 'England, France, the papacy and the Flemish succession', *Journal of Medieval History*, 2 (1976), 339-64. A study of Edward's continuing ambitions in the years following the Treaty of Brétigny.

E. Perroy, *The Hundred Years War* (first pub. in French 1945, Engl. trans. New York: Capricorn Books, 1965). An excellent overview of events and causes, which helpfully includes much on French politics.

C. J. Phillpotts, 'John of Gaunt and English policy towards France 1389-95', *Journal of Medieval History*, 16 (1990), 363-86. Emphasises the role of Gaunt's personal ambitions in the complex peace negotiations of these years.

A. J. Pollard, *John Talbot and the War in France, 1427-1453* (London: Royal Historical Society, 1983). Clearly reveals the seriousness with which the English took their interests in France after the Treaty of Troyes.

M. Prestwich, *Edward I* (London: Eyre Methuen, 1988). Provides accounts of Edward I's policies towards France and Scotland.

P. E. Russell, *The English Intervention in Spain and Portugal in the time of Edward III and Richard II* (Oxford: Clarendon Press, 1955). A very detailed account of this important theatre of war.

J. W. Sherborne, 'Indentured retinues and English expeditions to France 1369-89', *EHR*, 79 (1964), 718-46. Says much about English war policies as well as military organisation.

J. W. Sherborne, 'The battle of La Rochelle and the war at sea 1372-75', *BIHR*, 42 (1969), 17-29. Emphasises the significance of the war at sea in the later fourteenth century.

J. Sumption, *The Hundred Years War* (London: Faber, 1990). First of a projected multi-volume account of the war, densely packed with information.

G. Templeman, 'Edward III and the beginnings of the Hundred Years War', *TRHS*, fifth series, 2 (1952), 69-88. One of the major statements on the subject, stressing the intractable nature of the problems.

G. L. Thompson, *Paris and its People under English Rule: the Anglo-Burgundian Regime 1420–1436* (Oxford: Clarendon Press, 1991). Parallels Allmand's study of Normandy and Vale's study of Gascony in this period.

J. A. Tuck, 'Richard II and the Hundred Years War', in *Politics and Crisis in Fourteenth-Century England*, ed. J. Taylor and W. Childs (Gloucester: Alan Sutton, 1990), pp. 117–31. An important contribution to the debate on Richard's peace policies.

M. G. A. Vale, *English Gascony 1399–1453* (Oxford: Clarendon Press, 1970). A significant study of English rule and policies in Gascony in the fifteenth century.

M. G. A. Vale, *Charles VII* (London: Eyre Methuen, 1974). Explains Charles's policies and eventual success against the English.

M. G. A. Vale, *The Angevin Legacy 1250–1340* (Oxford: Blackwell, 1990). A scholarly and stimulating study of Gascony which sees the reign of Edward I as a major turning-point in Anglo-French relations, linking it to the outbreak of war in 1337–40.

R. Vaughan, *Philip the Bold* (1963), *John the Fearless* (1966), *Philip the Good* (1970) and *Charles the Bold* (1973), all London: Longman. Invaluable studies of the vital role which the dukes of Burgundy played in Anglo-French relations from the late 1360s onwards.

M. Wade-Labarge, *Gascony. England's First Colony 1204–1453* (London: Hamish Hamilton, 1980). A more 'popular' account than Vale provides but one which looks at the significance of Gascony over almost the entire period of its tenure.

S. L. Waugh, *England in the Reign of Edward III* (Cambridge University Press, 1991). A more wide-ranging study than Ormrod's, giving greater stress to the problems of war finance.

B. P. Wolffe, *Henry VI* (London: Eyre Methuen, 1981). A biography which is particularly interesting on Henry's attitude to the war and on the attempts to reach a settlement in the 1440s.

J. H. Wylie and W. T. Waugh, *The Reign of Henry the Fifth* (3 vols, Cambridge University Press, 1914–29). Until Allmand's biography of Henry V in the Eyre Methuen series appears this remains the fullest account of this king's ambitions and activities in France.

GLOSSARY

allod – an area held in absolute ownership, without the need to pay homage or other services to a superior lord

appanage – an extensive territory granted to sustain members of usually the cadet branches of the French royal family

appeals – an approach to a higher authority for deliverance from the adverse decision of a lower authority. In the context of Anglo-French relations, the approach by the vassals of the English king's lands in France to the French king, whom they saw as exercising superior legal jurisdiction

Chambre des Comptes – the French crown's equivalent of the English Exchequer

chevauchée – a campaign which took the form of an extensive raid through enemy territory, from the French *chevaucher* – to ride

Exchequer – the principal financial department of the English crown, which both received and paid out monies

fief – an area of land, with accompanying rights stemming from its tenure, which is held of a lord usually for military service

homage – the formal and public acknowledgement of allegiance to a lord, whereby a tenant or vassal admits his obligations to the king or lord of whom he holds land

liege homage – homage whereby the vassal admits his obligation to pay full feudal service (including military service) to his lord

parlement – the supreme court of the French king at Paris, which developed from the reign of Louis IX onwards

propriété – full ownership; the possession of an exclusive title to land

ressort – the right to have the final decision in appeals; supreme judicial authority

Salic Law – the alleged fundamental law of the French monarchy whereby females were excluded from the succession to the throne, supposedly derived from the laws of the Salian Franks of the fifth and sixth centuries

simple homage – homage which admits that the land is held of a lord, but which does not oblige the vassal to pay the full range of feudal services

sovereignty – the exercise of supreme power, authority or dominion, which does not admit of any outside control

usufruct – the right of temporary possession of property, which does not damage or diminish any of the rights of the full owner

vassal – someone who holds land from a lord on condition of allegiance

Wardrobe – a part of the royal household developed under Henry III and Edward I as a smaller and more flexible financial office than the Exchequer; often used by thirteenth- and fourteenth-century kings when on campaign for the payment of troops and of other wartime expenses

INDEX

Index

Index

Gloucester, Humphrey, duke of, 10, 110–11, 114, 125
Gloucester, Thomas, duke of, 83, 86
government records, 21–2, 24, 31
Grandes Chroniques, 49
Grant, A., 147–8
Gray, Sir Thomas, *Scalacronica*, 10, 13, 142
Green, J. R., *History of the English People*, 25
Guesclin, Bertrand du, 13, 71
Guînes, 66, 68, 70; negotiations at (1352–4), 64–5

Hainault, county of, 125–6
Hainault, John of, 12
Hainault, Philippa of, queen of England, wife of Edward III, 11–12, 70
Hainault, William, count of, 48, 54–5
Halidon Hill, battle of (1333), 142
Hall, Edward, 16–17
Hallam, H. E., *View of the State of Europe*, 15, 24
Hanson, Christopher, 11, 13–14, 17, 19
Hapsburg dynasty, 118
Harcourt, Geoffrey de, 63
Harfleur, 80, 97–9 *passim*, 112
Hearne, Thomas, 21
Henry II, king of England, 1, 32, 62
Henry III, king of England, 2, 34, 36–8 *passim*, 92
Henry IV, king of England, 89–94 *passim*, 147–8
Henry V, king of England, 4, 7, 86, 122, 133, 135, 148, 152–4 *passim*; as Prince of Wales, 92–3; as Regent of France, 107–8; campaigns in France, 94–109 *passim*; dealings with allies, 128; in Normandy, 99–100, 105–6, 108–9; historical treatment of, 10, 18, 21, 23, 26, 29
Henry VI, king of England, 4, 95, 104–5, 109, 111, 114–16 *passim*, 119, 133, 154
Henry VII (Tudor), king of England, 117–19 *passim*
Henry VIII, king of England, 119–21, 149

Henry IV (of Navarre), king of France, 18, 120
Henry, Robert, *History of Great Britain*, 23
Henry (of Trastamara), king of Castile, 71–3 *passim*, 79, 82, 125–6
heralds, 12, 19
Historia Roffensis, 53
Holinshed, Raphael, 16–17
Holland, county of, 70, 125–6
Hume, David, *History of England*, 23
Hundred Years War, use of term, 6, 24, 30–1, 122, 152–3; Second Hundred Years War, 1, 4
Hungerford, Walter Lord, 10

Ireland, 77, 87
Isabella, queen of England, wife of Edward II, 42, 44, 46–8 *passim*
Isabella, queen of England, wife of Richard II, 86–7, 90
Isabella, queen of France, wife of Charles VI, 103

James I, king of Scotland, 147–8
James IV, king of Scotland, 149
James VI, king of Scotland (James I, king of England), 138
Jeanne, d'Evreux, daughter of Louis X of France, 45, 64
Joan, of Arc, 18, 25, 105, 111
John, king of England, 1, 33–4
John I, king of France, 45
John II, king of France, 59, 63–7 *passim*, 96–7, 145–6
Joinville, Jean, 38
Juliers, margrave of, 54–5

Keen, M. H., 111, 113
Knighton, Henry, 62
Knollys, Sir Robert, 76

La Réole, 75
La Rochelle, 41, 75, 79, 80, 82–3
Lancaster, Henry, earl (later duke) of, 61–2
Lancaster, John (of Gaunt), duke of, 76, 79, 82, 83–7 *passim*, 125, 129, 134

189

Index